The Writ of Liberty

No free man shall be taken
or imprisoned or dispossessed
or outlawed or banished
or in any way destroyed
nor will we go upon him
nor send upon him
except by the lawful judgement of his peers
and by the law of the land.

Magna Carta Chapter 39, 1215 A.D.

Rex vicecomiti saluten.
Praecipimus tibi quod distringas A.
per terras et catalla sua in balliva tua,
ita quod *habeas corpus* ejus coram justiciariis
nostris, tali die ad respondendum B.

Habeas Corpus, 1220 A.D.
(see Index)

Forward to the 2006 Edition: In its 800-year history, the writ of habeas corpus ad subjiciendum et recipiendum has evolved as one of the principal instruments holding executive power accountable to the rule of law. Whether stated by Charles I or Bush II, the argument for executive power has remained the same – in times of crisis and emergency it is the executive's singular responsibility to protect and preserve the nation. This responsibility might, it is argued, entail uses of power that would not be acceptable in more tranquil times. The usual response to aggressive executive authority has also been the same – the executive power, in its effort to protect the nation, must not use measures that destroy the individual rights that define the nation's character as one embodying law and freedom. The argument between these positions has arisen many times in both England and the United States.

The current debate, inspired by actions of the George W. Bush administration, has had the effect of giving contemporary relevance to the monographs presented here, both long out-of-print and available only in court, university, and law school libraries. Commencing with the landmark case of Fay v. Noia, 372 US 391 (1963), the first monograph has been cited in decisions of the U.S. Supreme Court when the opinion writer, such as J. Brennan in *Fay*, thought that a reference to the writ's English constitutional development was called for. Recently, in 2002-2004, it was used in the development of the combined *Amici* briefs of the New York and American Civil Liberties Union for some of the so-called Guantanamo Cases: See: Rumsfeld, Secretary of Defense v. Padilla, 542 US 426 (2004)[1], as well as the ACLU, et al, *Amici* Brief in Hamdi v. Rumsfeld, 124 S.Ct. 2633 (2004). Earlier, in 1966, it was used in the Plaintiff's Brief, Martinez v. Immigration and Naturalization Service, 229 F.3rd 906, no. 001911. Similarly, the study of the *American Reception* has been found useful in explaining our colonial and early national history and problems, such as those arising from the writ of habeas corpus operating within

---

[1] www.nyclu.org/padilla_amicus_appeal_072903.html

a dual court system, federal environment – a problem area for decisional finality that very much concerned the Rhenquist Court.[2]

The first monograph here, on English development, is a reprint of the 1960 original, published by Oklahoma State University. I thought it best to change nothing from pagination to substance since it has been cited in judicial opinions, briefs, and scholarly articles.[3] However, there have been substantial additions to the American monograph in an effort to make its narrative more clearly relevant to the 21st century problems arising from Bush administration policies and practices.

The great American savant George Santayana wisely observed, "Those who cannot remember the past are condemned to repeat it." I offer these studies as a reminder of our history as revealed in the evolution of the Writ of Liberty, and because I believe that the lessons of that history apply clearly and directly to the serious problems Americans face in the 21st century.

Robert Searles Walker
rwalker_1@msn.com
San Antonio, Texas
June 2006

---

[2] http://law.onecle.com/constitution/article-I/51-habeas-corpus-suspension.html.

[3] For example: Dallin H. Oaks, "Legal History in the High Court – Habeas Corpus," Michigan Law Rev., vol. 64, no.3 (January 1966), pp. 451-472.

This work is dedicated
to my Grandchildren

Elise Christine Voorhis
Robert Justin Voorhis

The generation in whose hands now rest
the quality, liberty, and destiny
of our nation

HABEAS CORPUS WRIT OF LIBERTY

English and American Origins and Development

Being a Reprint of

The Constitutional and Legal Development
Of Habeas Corpus as the Writ of Liberty

Together with 2006 Revised edition

The American Reception of
the Writ of Liberty

Robert Searles Walker, Ph.D.
Professor Emeritus, Trinity University
San Antonio, Texas

BookSurge LLC
An Amazon.com Company

Library of Congress Control Number 2006906118
ISBN 1-4196-4478-5

The Constitutional and Legal Development of Habeas Corpus was first published by Oklahoma State University in 1960 as Vol. 57, No. 9 of the Arts and Sciences Studies.
Copyright © by Robert S(earles) Walker, 1960, all rights reserved.
Library of Congress Catalog: H31.053, no.3

The American Reception of the Writ of Liberty was first published by Oklahoma State University in 1961 as No. 1, Political Science Research Reports, A Monograph Series.
Copyright © by Robert S(earles) Walker, 1961, all rights reserved.
Library of Congress Catalog: KF9011.Z9.W34

CONTENTS

Forward 2006 edition

The Constitutional and Legal Development Of Habeas Corpus as the Writ of Liberty

Preface

PREFACE

Among the necessary conditions of individual life in society none stand higher than the realization in law and fact of the social interest in the physical security of the individual person. "The inviolability of the physical person," as Roscoe Pound stated, "is universally put first among the demands which the individual may make."[4] Positively this right of personal liberty is what Herbert Spencer simply termed "freedom of motion and locomotion." Its existence makes possible the completion of people as moral beings for it makes possible the implementation of their choices.[5] Except in those areas in which the law accepts a liability without fault, it underlies the entire body of Anglo-American law.

The right of personal liberty is more familiar and, perhaps, more meaningful when formulated in negative terms. Like many of the rights and privileges recognized in the Anglo-American tradition, its legal form is one of protection against, rather than the positive promotion of something. It is a "permissive" rather than an "enabling" right. It entails a guarantee "of non-interference while entrusting the fulfillment of interests to the private

---

[4]Roscoe Pound, "Interests of Personality," 28 *Harvard Law Review* (1915), at p.35; see also: Julius Stone, *The Province and Function of Law* (Harvard 1950), p.506 et seq.; Eugene Ehrlich, *Fundamental Principles of the Sociology of Law* (Harvard 1936), pp.360-362.

[5] Herbert Spencer, *Social Statics* (New York 1890), p.92, 130; William Ernest Hocking, *Present Status of the Philosophy of Law and of Rights* (Yale 1926), pp.86-88; W. Friedmann, *Legal Theory* (London 1949, 2nd ed.), pp.446-449.

resources of the individual."[6] In legal terms, the right of personal liberty means the right to be free from arbitrary seizure and detention, the right to be protected against restraint without a regular, recognized process of law intervening. This negative and narrow formulation may appear unsatisfying, but liberty must, indeed, mean absence of external restraints before it can mean anything better.[7]

The great genius of the Anglo-American tradition respecting the development of this right is that it has not been confined to the channels of philosophic speculation.[8] The claim has been expressed and pressed in terms of concrete legal standards and procedures. Most notably, the right of personal liberty is connected in both the legal and popular mind with procedure upon the writ of habeas corpus ad subjiciendum et recipiendum. The writ is simply a judicial command directed to a specific jailer directing him or her to produce a named prisoner together with the legal cause of detention in order that the legal warrant of detention might be examined. If the magistrate to whom the writ is returned finds no warrant in law, absolute discharge must follow. If reason exists, then the prisoner may be remanded to close custody or bailed, that is placed in constructive custody, pending a trial with date certain. The process is not about ultimate guilt or innocence, a matter commonly misunderstood. It is solely about the legal basis for a detention. The essence of habeas corpus is that it provides for a speedy and independent hearing on

---

[6] Ralph Barton Perry, *Realms of Value, A Critique of Human Civilization* (Harvard 1954), p.236.
[7] T.V. Smith and Eduard C. Lindeman, *The Democratic Way of Life* (New York 1951), p.44-45.
[8] Everett Dean Martin, *Liberty* (New York 1930), passim.

the merit of detention. Without it a person can simply "disappear" – be removed from civil society, without recourse or reason in law, indeed, often with no one noticing until it is too late.

However, a simple description is deceptive; it leaves crucial matters masked. The protection that the judiciary wields on behalf of the individual through the writ is primarily a protection against executive power, pre-eminent in medieval times, paramount in our own. A moment's reflection reveals that an effective habeas corpus assumes an independent judiciary operating within the context of a constitutional or limited state.[9] Here is the slippery slope for, inherently, the judiciary is the smallest and weakest branch of government. The chief executive has a monopoly of force and the power of initiative, legislators can access the public treasury and their constituencies, but the judicial power rests on the public's insistence upon the rule of law, its faith in the integrity of the court system, and its willingness and ability to use it. A judiciary without independence is just another specialized bureaucracy. If the public does not support it's independent power, then it has none. If it has none, then there is only an illusion, not the reality, of personal liberty – as Germans, Russians, Italians, Chileans, Iraqui, and many others have discovered in modern times.

The history of habeas corpus is, then, a major chapter in the evolution of the constitutional and democratic state. It is this chapter that I have attempted to write, and I have needed much help along the way. Many thanks are due Mr. Fred Bosco of the University of Michigan's Romance Language Department for his

---

[9] A.V. Dicey, *Introduction to the Study of The Law of the Constitution* (London 1950, 9th ed.), p.222.

assistance in deciphering the Norman-French, English-Latin mixture of the early Year Books, as well as the help of many skilled librarians at Michigan's superb law library. I must also thank Professors J.A.C. Grant and Foster Sherwood, both noted public law scholars at U.C.L.A., for their help and guidance when this monograph was in its first incarnation as a doctoral dissertation. Many may rightfully claim much credit for whatever merit exists. The shortcomings are exclusively my own.

Robert Searles Walker

CHAPTER I

The Early Medieval History of the Writ of Habeas Corpus

Part 1: The Legal and Constitutional Setting

The Twentieth century has witnessed a revolutionary expansion in the state's sphere of competence accompanied by a concomitant increase in its effective power. Permeating all areas of endeavor, its activities and spokesmen too frequently exalt the desideratum of efficiency at the expense of values which, at least in the constitutional order, ought to be of paramount and guiding influence. Thus, in the present period, effective protection of personal liberty occupies a prominent place in political and legal thought, and everyday experience with law enforcement accentuates the value of such procedural devices as the modern writ of habeas corpus.

However, as we move back into the period of Magna Carta to locate the origin and uses of habeas corpus we must note that comparable problems and procedures do not exist. State power did not completely overshadow all possible competitors nor were its instruments so sophisticated as to make possible even the capture of the mind. This was immediately reflected in the law of arrest. We find that it was as yet in a primitive state, and the problem of security from arbitrary arrest and imprisonment did not have the proportions which even the complaints embodied in the Great Charter suggested. Divorced from the power conflicts which raged round the throne, the common man had relatively little to fear. Commitment pending trial, except for appeals of homicide, was the exception rather than the rule. Costly incarceration was a bothersome responsibility for the sheriff, and in the closed community life of the Twelfth and Thirteenth centuries a simple surety system—bolstered by fear of outlawry—operated well enough.[1] To provide for such detention, pending judicial disposition, as was used, the law knew a series of writs which Maitland aptly labeled the "Liberty Group," and which were designed to secure release from commitment on bail and/or pledges.[2] These writs, *de homine replegiando*, mainprize, and *de odio et atia*, issued in the name of the king to his sheriff directing that a prisoner be bailed or replevied " . . . according to the custom of England, That we may hear no more clamour thereupon

---

1. Frederick Pollock and Frederick Maitland, *The History of English Law before the time of Edward I* (*London* 1898, 2nd ed.), Vol. II, pp. 582-585 (hereafter cited: Pollock and Maitland).
2. Frederic Maitland, "The History of the Register of Original Writs," *Select Essays in Anglo-American Law* (Boston 1908), Vol. II, pp. 583-592 (hereafter cited Select Essays).

for want of justice."[3] These writs issued out of Chancery as a matter of course and involved no preliminary judicial or administrative examination of the validity of the charge upon which the petitioner had been committed. There was, merely, a catalog of offenses which in that day were not thought of sufficient import to warrant incarceration pending trial.[4]

It is important to note in this period and, indeed, for quite some time in the future, no writ ran against the king; he was, after all the source of them. Arrest *per speciale mandatum domini Regis* was final, and no court would presume to release a man committed in these circumstances. To read such a power of release into the annals of the Middle Ages is to assume too perfect a separation of the executive and the judiciary. The courts were not independent; judges were still the king's very obedient servants.[5] Pollock and Maitland cite an instance in which a royal court invalidated in 1234 the king's outlawry of William Raleigh as a "memorable triumph for law over arbitrary power." But this was certainly exceptional. The triumph was political rather than legal in nature.[6] The court was simply the instrument recording a shift in power.

However there was a set of constitutional and legal values developing which pretended to describe procedural standards prevailing between the king and his subjects. These were dramatically put forward in Chapter 29 of the Great Charter:

> No free man shall be taken or imprisoned or dispossessed or outlawed, or banished, or in any way destroyed, nor will we go upon him, nor send upon him, except by the legal judgment of his peers and by the law of the land.[7]

How broad a social application this clause was to have is not entirely clear,[8] but the norms expressed were clearly the essence of a consti-

3. Sir Anthony Fitz-Herbert, *New Natura Brevium* (London 1793, Hale's annotated 9th ed.), p. 142.
4. For a detailed examination of the origins and uses of the writs of the liberty group see: Elsa de Haas, *Antiquities of Bail, Origin and Historical Development in Criminal Cases to the Year 1275* (New York 1940).
5. William S. Holdsworth, *A History of English Law* (Boston 1926), Vol. IX, p. 107.
6. *Pollock and Maitland*, Vol. II, p. 587.
7. William Sharp McKechnie, *Magna Carta, A Commentary on the Great Charter of King John* (Glasgow 1914 2nd ed). p. 375. In the original Charter of 1215 this chapter was numbered "39." In later editions it became "29." I will use the latter for sake of agreement with excerpts used later.
8. There are three distinct views on the social application of this chapter: (1) that "freeman" referred only to tenants-in-chief of the crown; (2) that the term had the same meaning as that found in the body of the common law; (3) that it referred to the liberties of the community at large. For these views see: (1) G. B. Adams, "The Origin of the English Constitution," 13 *American Historical Review* (1908) 229-244; G. M. Trevelyan, *History of England* (New York, 1954), Vol. I, p. 277; (2) Paul Vinogradoff, "Clause 39," in: Henry Elliot Malden, *Magna Carta Commemoration Essays* (London 1917), pp. 78-95; (3) J. E. A. Jolliffe, *The Constitutional History of Medieval England from the English Settlement to 1485* (London 1948, 2nd ed.), p. 261.
    The problem of social application was solved in the Fourteenth century when the term "freeman" gave way by statute to a simple "no man." See: 28 Edward III, c. 3, 1 *Statutes of the Realm* (1810) 345: "That no man of what [ever] estate or condition that he be shall be put . . ." (hereafter cited: Stat. Realm).

tutional order.[9]

This chapter meant several things to the Barons of Runnymede. First and foremost, it expressed their demand that a judgment must precede execution, and, moreover, that judgment be rendered by men of the proper sort.[10] The phrase "judgment of his peers," *judicium parium*, embodied one of the central maxims of feudal life: that no man, whatever his station, be judged by his inferiors.[11] Every man had his station and was constrained to remain within it. Just as fire rose because it was its nature to do so, this was the divinely established way. The barons were, in effect, protesting King John's frequent circumvention of accepted legal process. The principle involved seemed simple enough, but the application proved to be a most difficult and vexing problem for coming generations.

As another measure of safety the Barons demanded that not only must they have the benefit of prior judgment, but also that the judgment must have been given in accordance with the "law of the land." In the early period of the Charter *lex terrae* had a technical significance denoting the "law" or "proof" which was applicable to a certain judgment as rendered by a body of doomsmen. The "judgment" of the doomsmen was not a judgment in the modern usage. It was rather a finding that a *bona fides* dispute existed. Having such a judgment, the court could then prescribe according to well-known rules what proof (lex) was necessary to determine the ultimate questions of guilt and which of the disputants would have to "wage his law," that is, undertake the proof.[13] But when a man met his King in direct dispute, the judgment of peers was treated as a means to determine finally the issue, and thus "judgment" became the crucial "proof" rather than a medial finding of justified dispute.[14]

Whatever the specific procedure, it is clear that Chapter 29 was designed to provide a threefold protection to the subject. The persons and properties of the King's subjects were to be protected against his arbitrary action by the proviso that a judgment precede execution. Moreover, this judgment was to be made by men at least peers of the subject. And finally that the judgment was to emerge from proper and appropriate procedure.

9. Jolliffe, *op. cit.*, p. 260.
10. McKechnie, *op. cit.*, p. 376.
11. Like the problem of the scope to be given the term "freeman," it was not altogether clear how strictly status-equality had to be observed. See: *Pollock and Maitland*, Vol. I, p. 409; Vinogradoff, *op. cit.*, p. 90; McKechnie, *op. cit.*, p. 377-379. This particularly was a problem when royal judges of low personal rank presided over trials involving their social superiors. See: F. M. Powicke, "Per Iudicium Parium vel per Legem Terrae," in: Malden, *op. cit.*, pp. 96-121, at p. 99; Faith Thompson, *Magna Carta, Its Role in the Making of the English Constitution, 1300-1629* (Minneapolis 1948). In the end, however, the authority of the royal courts and judges prevailed. See: Frederic Maitland, *The Constitutional History of England* (London 1908), pp. 169-171.
13. *Pollock and Maitland*, Vol. II, pp. 599-604.
14. Powicke, *op. cit.*, p. 100

In the course of the Fourteenth century these demands acquired new guises. The basic ideas remained the same, but the procedural concepts accompanying them changed taking on a more modern look. These changes came about largely as a result of the political turmoil characteristic of the period from Richard III to Henry VIII, turmoil which caused the monarchs to rely heavily on special commissions and courts outside of the regular common law system for the administration and execution of their policies. The conciliar court system which resulted possessed a more flexible and summary procedure and, in some cases, a more effective remedy than did the common law courts. The contrasts between the authority and effectiveness of the two systems of legal administration gave rise to considerable mutual antagonism.[15]

During the Fourteenth century the objections of the common lawyers centered on the Romanesque procedure characteristically utilized by the conciliar courts. In particular, they were disturbed by the fact that the conciliar courts frequently instituted actions against treason or felony on the basis of "suggestion" or "information." This procedure ran counter to the use of the indicting jury which was becoming increasingly popular in all types of cases at the common law, and it was clearly recognized that such practices were fraught with the dangers of arbitrary and malicious persecution in the guise of legal prosecution.[16] The common lawyers objected also to the form of examination procedure used in Council and Chancery. Both had adopted the oath *ex officio* from canonical procedure, and the oath committed the party being investigated to answer truthfully all questions put to him before he was given any indication of the charge. In effect, the oath procedure, as used by the conciliar courts, initiated a sort of roving commission to ferret out evil-doing and crush it. Overlooking the fact that the common law had very little to recommend it as far as protecting the interests of the accused was concerned,[17] the common lawyers attacked the conciliar procedure as "fishing interrogatories *viva voce*."

A series of acts passed between 1330 and 1370 record clearly the hostility toward these practices as well as the process which was being asserted as "within the form of the Charter." For example, the Act of 1352 maintained that:

> Where as it is contained in the Great Charter . . . that none shall be imprisoned nor put out of his freehold, nor of his liberties, or free customs, unless it be by the law of the land; it is accorded, assented and established, that from henceforth none shall be taken by petition or suggestion made to . . . the King, or to his council,

15. Holdsworth, *History*, Vol. I, pp. 266-270.
16. *Ibid.*, Vol. IX, pp. 236-241.
17. James F. Steven, *History of the Criminal Law of England* (London 1883), Vol. I, p. 350.

unless it be by indictment of good and lawful people of the same neighborhood where such deeds be done, in due manner, or by process made by writ original at the common law; nor that none be out of his liberties nor of his freeholds, unless he be duly brought in to answer, and forjudged of the same by the course of the law; and if anything be done against the same, it shall be redressed and holden for none.[18]

But as always in the Medieval period it is far easier to get the law declared than to secure its enforcement and especially so when the act tends to curb the prerogative. The conciliar courts continued to use the procedures so convenient for kings attempting to consolidate and stabilize their reigns. And Parliament continued to petition for the restriction or prohibition of such practices.[19] The remaining statutes add nothing significant to the above with the exception of a tacit admittance of defeat.[20]

Though the principle of *judicium parium vel per legem terrae* was evolving into a set of fairly explicit legal prescriptions throughout the Fourteenth century, it was far from being secured. Indeed, the annals of the entire turbulent period from John Plantagenet through the reign of Lancaster and York are filled with accounts of arbitrary imprisonments, convictions and executions as the contending factions vied for power. A favorite device for circumventing ordinary lawful process was the conviction on the basis that the alleged offense, being "notoriously well known," required no regular judgment of peers, and, similarly, indictment and appeal could be dispensed with.[21] The critical issues of the period were not, of course, issues of legality, but rather of sheer power.

Only the first faltering steps along the road of constitutionalism had been taken. The courts could not yet claim independence from executive intervention, and political power remained unlimited except in the sense that opposing autocratic forces sometimes balanced one another. The liberties of an Englishman counted for naught if he were caught in the struggle. Yet the main lines of the rule of law and due process had been marked out by the Thirteenth and Fourteenth centuries for succeeding generations. No man, not even a king, should be above the law. Nor should he be arrested or committed without cause. He ought to be indicted by his "neighbors" in grand jury assembled, not by secret

---

18. 25 Edward III, st. 5, ca. 4, 1 *Stat. Realm* (1810) 321. See: Harold Potter, *An Historical Introduction to English Law and Its Institutions* (London 1948, 3rd ed.), pp. 139ff.
19. Holdsworth, *History*, Vol. I, pp. 266-268.
20. 37 Edward III, ca. 18 (1363), I *Stat. Realm* (1810) 382. See also: 38 Edward III, st. 1, ca. 9, I *Stat. Realm* (1810) 384; 5 Edward III, ca. 9 (1332), I *Stat. Realm* (1810) 267; 28 Edward III, ca; 3 (1354), *Stat. Realm* (1810) 345; 31 Edward III, st. 4, ca. 16, I *Stat. Realm* (1810) 362; 42 Edward III, ca. 13 (1368), I *Stat. Realm* (1810) 388.
21. T. F. T. Pluckett, "The Origins of Impeachment," in: Royal Historical Society, *Transactions*, 4th series, Vol. XXXIV (London 1942), pp. 47-71; Thompson, *op. cit.*, p. 74

"information" or malicious "suggestion." He should have the right to appear at his trial—not be tried *in absentia* and convicted by "notoriety."[22] And as trial by jury, with the assistance of *peine forte et dure,* replaced older forms it became associated with the concept of judgment by peers according to the law of the land and took its place on the catalog of procedural rights.[23] Finally the judgment delivered must have resulted from this due process before execution could properly take place. All these claims—and they are as yet claims pressing, not secured—make up what later ages were to call the "immemorial rights of Englishmen which runneth back until the mind of man knoweth not to the contrary."

This, then, constituted the milieu of legal practices and constitutional ideas which surrounded the birth and infancy of habeas corpus. But the writ did not spring full grown from the fertile womb of early judicial inventiveness. It had a definite role and place in the over-all legal structure, but its connection with the great ideas of lawful process developing during this period was only tenuous. The construction of a direct bond between the writ and the ideas of which the Charter was symbol was to be the task of a later period. In its earliest period the writ of habeas corpus was a rather simple judicial command with a humble but necessary role.

Part 2: The Beginnings of Habeas Corpus Twelfth and Thirteenth Centuries

It is dangerous to generalize about legal practice in Twelfth century England, but there does appear at the end of the century evidence indicating that a rudimentary habeas corpus was in use. I hesitate to use the word "writ" in this connection because it has a connotation of formal definition which I do not think can be warrantably ascribed to the practice of which we have evidence. Two court orders appear in 1199 which command one party to "have" another named party appear before the court at Westminster.[24] A few years later, however, the *Coram Rege Rolls* yield a definite habeas corpus, and there is nothing in the reported version of *Tyrel's Case* (1214) to indicate that the form of the court's command was novel or unusual:

22. I do not mean to imply that a man was given the right to appear and defend himself as in modern criminal procedure. The right asserted was mere physical presence. See: 42 Edward III, ca. 3 (1368), 1 *Stat. Realm* 388.
23. Holdsworth, *History,* Vol. I, pp. 153ff.
24. Prior of Saint Fredericks case (1199) and Adam de Cardvil's case (1199), in: Francis Palgrave (ed.), *Rotuli Curiae Regis* (London 1835), Vol. II. p. 178 With the original abbreviations spelled out the court orders read: "Prior de Sancta Fredeswida dixit quod summonitus fuit apud Westminster habiturus quendam clericum Sahier iuri peritur et quod ipse non est sub potestate sua nec aliquid vult facere" And: "Adam de Cardvil, et predeptum est eidem Valtero quod tanc habest Wimarcem uxorem suam ibi."

The sheriff was commanded to have the body of Baldwin Tyrel before the king . . . to answer Ranulf of Devonsby . . . touching an appeal they made against him . . . (for) denouncing the king's death, and to summon the said Ranulf . . . to be there to prosecute their appeal against him.[25]

Back of these orders I cannot go. The ultimate origin of the process is a subject of speculation. William S. Church, for example, feels that the habeas corpus might have derived from unknown Norman process or even indirectly from the Roman praetorian edict *de libero homine exibendo*.[26] In the absence of documentary evidence, however, I am inclined to believe that the origin of the process lies in the structure of the legal language itself. Literally habeas corpus means "have the body," and cast in the imperative mode by a court it is quite conceivable that natural usage could, in time, evolve into discrete process. Interpreted thus, the phrase habeas corpus becomes merely an expression of the directive power of a royal judge trying to conclude some litigation.

By the first quarter of the Thirteenth century, however, the evidence indicates strongly that the general judicial command has become a more or less settled process, that is, a writ, used for specific reasons. In the *Curia Regis Rolls* for 1219-1220 we find specific court orders directed to the sheriff in the following fashion:

Praeceptum fuit vicecomiti quod haberet corpus Ricardi de Brom ad respondendum Radulfo Table . . .[27]

The court, in these instances, is commanding a royal officer to produce a certain party before the court in order that he might respond to an appeal instituted against him, or in order that he might hear and understand the court's award. Similar entries in the *Memoranda* and *Plea Rolls* of Henry III indicate that a habeas corpus command is being used quite widely during the Thirteenth century.[28]

The major purpose for which the command issued was simply the production of parties without whom legal proceedings, short of outlawry, could not be terminated. Habeas corpus was part of the mesne process for the production of parties before the court. It was a kind of forcible summons. Bracton's *Note-Book* contains many references to

---

25. Frederic W. Maitland (ed.), *Select Pleas of the Crown, 1200-1225* (London 1888). The original read: ". . . . quod haberet . . . corpus Baldwenni. . . ad respondendum. . ., et quod summoneret ipsos Rannulfum. . . ad prosequendam." (hereafter cited: Select Crown Pleas, 1200-1225).

26. *A Treatise on the Writ of Habeas Corpus* (San Francisco 1893, 3rd ed.), pp. 2ff.

27. *Curia Regis Rolls*, Vol. VIII, 3-4 Henry III (1220) (London 1938), p. 308. The original read: ". . . quod haberet. . . corpus Baldwenni. . . ad prosequendam."

28. Hilary Jenkinson and Beryl E. R. Formoy (eds.), *Select Cases in the Exchequer of Pleas, 1216-1272* (London 1932), pp. xxxiii, lvii-lviii (hereafter cited: Select Exchequer Cases.)

habeas corpus in this role.[29] Indeed, Bracton's scheme of personal actions included habeas corpus as an integral part: (1) Summons, (2) Attachment by pledges, (3) Attachment by better pledges, (4) Habeas Corpus, (5) Distraint of all goods and chattels in three varieties of stringency, and (6) Exaction or outlawry.[30] This particular use of habeas corpus disappeared by 1267 in the general abbreviation of process in personal actions. Hengham's *Fet Asaver,* written sometime after Bracton's *Note-Book* but before 1267, shows that the habeas corpus command had been eliminated as a separate step and now appeared as an integral part of the first writ of distraint.[31] However, its elimination as a separate step did not eradicate its unique phraseology:

> Rex vicecomiti salutem. Praecipimus tibi guod distringas A. per terras et catalla sua in balliva tua, ita quod habeas corpus eius coram justiciariis nostris, etc., tali die ad respondendum B. . . [32]

Moreover, the elimination of habeas corpus as a step in the mesne process of personal actions did not remove the writ altogether from the legal scene as a separate entity.

In other words, though the writ's principal function in the first part of the Thirteenth century seems to have been as part of mesne process in personal actions, this was not its only role. *Tyrel's Case* was not a personal action, but a criminal complaint.[33] And there is no good reason to doubt that the writ served as a means of getting parties before the courts in a variety of other circumstances throughout the Thirteenth century. This is particularly persuasive in view of the fact that immediately upon entering the Fourteenth century the *Year Books* indicate such uses. For example, in *Adman's Case* (1313) a writ of habeas corpus was issued commanding the production of a party so that he could show cause why an agreement had not been executed.[34] In *Isabel's Case* (1313) the writ was issued to compel a party to answer an action in progress,[35] and in the case of *Smythe v. The Abbot of Preaux* (1313) habeas corpus was used to secure the presence of a party who had simply ignored summons.[36]

---

29. Henri de Bracton. *Note-Book, A Collection of Cases decided in the King's Courts during the Reign of Henry III,* edited by Frederic Maitland (London 1887), Vol. II, pl. 526, 527, 1370, 1376, 1407, 1408, 1420, 1421, 1426.
30. George E. Woodbime, *Four Thirteenth Century Law Tracts* (New Haven 1910), p. 10; *Pollock and Maitland,* Vol. II, p. 593.
31. *Ibid.,* pp. 10-12.
32. *Ibid.,* Hengham's *Fet Asaver,* pp. 53-115, at p. 91. There are many other entries in the *Fet Asaver* evidencing this practice; for example see p. 85 where the form runs: ". . .et quod hebeas corpora eorum coram iusticiariis nostris. . . ad faciendam iuratum illam. . .", and at p. 103 where it reads: ". . quod habeas corpora . . ad faciendam . . ea ad audiendum iudicium. . . " The *Judicium Essoniorum* also reproduced in Woodbine agrees with the *Fet Asaver* in its description of this abbreviated process. See. *Ibid.,* pp. 116-142, at p. 116.
33. *Supra,* p. 22.
34. William Craddock Bolland (ed.), *Year Books of Edward II, 6 Edward II, 1313* (London 1927), p. 146 (hereafter cited: Bolland, Year Book, 1313).
35. *Ibid,* p. 144.
36. Bolland, *Year Book 1313,* p. 22.

Additionally for the last part of the Thirteenth century and certainly by the first part of the Fourteenth, the writ acquired a new function not altogether unrelated to those of which I have been speaking. Not only was it being used to gather parties involved in the suit directly, but also to gather parties necessary to aid the court in arriving at a judgment. This is mentioned in Bracton's *De Legibus et Consuetudinibus Angliae* which, if we have the original text, would place this use as early as the mid-Thirteenth century.[37] At any rate habeas corpus was being used to gather juries by the Fourteenth century.[38] These juries were not, of course, the trial juries of more modern times. Rather they were bodies of twelve "lawful" men who were knowledgable of local conditions and were to give a verdict on whether forcible disseisin had taken place with regard to disputed property. In a later case Judge Littleton described this jury gathering process thus: ". . . in a plea in the Common Pleas when the parties are at issue, the process is venire facias, habeas corpora, and distress; and if the habeas corpora is wanting it is error; but in the King's Bench the practice is different, for there it shall be venire facias and distress and not habeas corpora.[39] Similarly this plural form of the habeas corpus was part of the process of gathering the four knights to determine questions of best title on the Grand Inquest.[40]

Although this is far from as full account of the earliest history of habeas corpus as one could wish, the writ's position and role are fairly clear. It was not an original writ, that is it did not mark the commencement of an action. Rather it was resorted to when preliminary process such as summons had failed to produce the desired party. Habeas corpus, at this stage, was a very versatile process in that it could issue against any party whether in custody or not, or to any person who might have custody of the desired party whether public or private. The specific reasons for its issuance might be the judges' desire to have a party hear the judgment of the court, to respond to an action then being heard in the court, or to prosecute an appeal instituted in the court.[41] Finally, it is important to note that this was the period when the law was making a slow separation of the notions and procedures re-

37. Travers Twiss (ed. & trans), *Henrici de Bracton, De Legibus et Consuetudinibus Angliae* (London 1878-1883), Vol. IV, p. 9.
38. John P. Collas and Theodore F. T. Plucknett (eds.), *Year Books of Edward II, 1319* (London 1953), p. 66 (hereafter cited: Collas, Year Book, 1319).
39. M. Hemmant (ed.), *Select Cases in the Exchequer Chamber Before all the Justices of England*, Vol. II, 1461-1509 (London 1948), p. 179 (hereafter cited: Hemmant, Exchequer Chamber Cases); See also: N. Neilson (ed.), *Year Books of Edward IV, 1470* (London 1930), pp. 134ff, 168-170 (herafter cited: Neilson, Year Book, 1470).
40. Fitz-Herbert, *New Natura Brevium*, p. 1.
41. This last use occurred in the sequel to Tyrel's Case, *supra*, p. 11, and note 25. As noted the writ first issued against Tyrel ad respondendum. Then when the appellors themselves failed to appear on summons to prosecute their appeal, a writ of habeas corpus ad prosequendum appellum suum was issued. Finally the court had to issue *alias* (second) writs as it was found that both the appellee and the appellors were in custody. See: *Select Crown Pleas*, 1200-1225, pp. 67ff and 75.

lating to proof and judgment, a separation exemplified, for example, in the growing use of fact-declaring juries. Habeas corpus very early formed an association with the probative side of procedure and maintained that tie throughout its history.

The connection of habeas corpus with the liberty of the subject was by no means as proximate as later ages assumed, but there did exist an underlying connection. A man could not be secure if legal proceedings affecting him could be instituted and terminated in his absence. Indeed a system permitting this would be highly destructive of individual security in both body and goods. There is, in other words, a social interest here in simply being aware of official declarations of rights and obligations, rewards and punishments, and the English legal system recognized this interest in a number of ways. The courts were, for example, extremely hesitant to procede in an action at law in the absence of any of the necessary parties to it. Indeed, this might be cited as one of the outstanding characteristics of the system, and an appreciation of this hesitancy is certainly necessary to a full understanding of the tedious mesne process of early actions or the labyrinthine law of essoins. And it is in this context that early habeas corpus connects with personal security and liberty. The writ was one of many means to secure adequate representation of contending interests, for without such representation, justice could not be done.

Part 3: The Writ of Habeas Corpus from 1300 A. D. to the Mid-Sixteenth Century

As we move into this later period of the writ's development many changes become manifest which will have an impact on our process. As already noted, the notions of due process at the common law were becoming more explicit until they took fairly definite form in the mid-Fourteenth century. But even as due process ideas developed, the old freedom from arrest and commitment pending judicial settlement was being eroded away. As the population grew and became more mobile, as towns became cities, the personal factor which lay at the foundation of the old surety system began to disintegrate. Already in the early Fourteenth century a medium-sized English town could boast of from three to four thousand inhabitants, while a few major trading centers such as London were becoming the Gothams of their day. We see the impact of this changing society on the development of the jury; no longer do the twelve good and lawful men know all that transpires in their communities. More important for our purposes is the impact of these changes on the law of arrest, detention, and bailment. A new stringency is found which did not exist in earlier days. As the intimacy of the small medieval community gave way to the anonymity of a greater society, the list of non-bailable offenses grew longer and longer. This meant that not only would it be more difficult for the malefactor to escape the clutches of the law, but also that there would be greater possibility of extended commitment without due process administered by the courts of common law.

At the same time these changes were taking place, the control over the administration of justice was slowly being centralized. In both civil and criminal matters the royal courts were assuming ascendancy over the multitude of special jurisdictions, while the royal magistrature evolved and perfected a variety of processes by which their superiority could be asserted.[42] Old and new forms of the writ of habeas corpus were, in part, the results of this evolving legal and social order, and, in part, instruments by which the restructuring was advanced.

By way of elaborating this last point, I want to examine two theses advanced by Professor Jenks in his pioneering article on habeas corpus.[43] Not discovering writs of habeas corpus in the documents of the Fourteenth century, Jenks asserted that the apparent disappearance of the writ after the Thirteenth century could be explained by the fact that the writ was for a time masquerading as part of the *capias* series of writs. As he expressed it, " . . . we find that, under the more familiar name of Capias, the writ of Habeas Corpus plays a normal part in almost every personal action."[44] If this thesis were true it would mean that the famous writ of liberty was in its earlier period a process of arrest!

This thesis has already been the subject of some examination. John C. Fox reasoned, correctly I think, that the two processes, habeas corpus and capias, while they might sometimes have the same effect, were different in kind.[45] The capias series were definitely writs of arrest to force satisfaction of judgment, while the habeas corpus was simply an order to produce the body at court for any one of a variety of reasons. The execution of the habeas corpus might have entailed, true enough, an arrest by the sheriff commanded to produce the body, but the writ did not necessarily involve arrest. Mr. Fox's arguments are very persuasive in this connection. But what really destroys the Jenks' thesis is the simple fact that writs of habeas corpus do appear in the records of the period. Some have already been noted from the Year Books of Edward II for 1313.[46] And there are more. For example, in 1359 the Common

42. See: F. W. Pollock, "The King's Peace in the Middle Ages," 2 *Select Essays* 403; Edward Jenks, *Law and Politics in the Middle Ages* (London 1919), Chaps. 3, 4.
43. Edward Jenks, "The Story of Habeas Corpus," 2 *Select Essays* 531-549.
44. *Ibid.*, p. 536.
45. John C. Fox, "The Process of Imprisonment at Common Law," 39 *Law Quarterly Review* (Jan. 1923) 58.
46. *Supra*, p. 14.

Bench issued a habeas corpus to the Sheriff of London to secure a party imprisoned by that official.[47] Again around 1360 we find a habeas corpus issued from King's Bench in order to secure a party imprisoned for debt so that he could appear in an action before that court.[48] We have then, examples at the beginning of the century, toward the middle, and the Year Books of Richard II yield one for the latter part of the Fourteenth century.[49] Moreover, later cases indicate that the court did not confuse the capias and habeas corpus writs.[50]

The second, and more important, thesis advanced by Professor Jenks is that the writ of habeas corpus was not used to test the validity of commitments until the Sixteenth century.[51] I find evidence indicating that a form of habeas corpus connected with such a test or inquiry was taking form in the first part of the Fourteenth century. A new form of the writ came into use during this period the very wording of which gives a hint as to its purpose. This new form was the habeas corpus cum causa captis et detentionis, or as it was commonly referred to, corpus cum causa. That this new form was being used to inquire into the warrant or regularity of imprisonment is, I think, indicated by one of the first cases in which it appears. In 1341 the Chancery directed by a corpus cum causa that a petitioner be produced before the judges because it appeared by his petition that he ought not to have been imprisoned.[52] Subsequently in 1351 an action appears in which the writs of habeas corpus and audita querela were used together.[53]. This latter writ permitted a party against whom judgment had been entered to re-open the case on ground of falsification of evidence or new evidence. In the present instance, for example, a recognitor claimed that he had been released from the balance of his obligation and could not therefore be sued in execution of debt. Essentially, then, his complaint was unjust commitment.

It seems reasonably clear to me that this new form was something different from what we have encountered before. The words "cum causa captis et detentionis" undoubtedly had the same significance as the phrases "ad respondendum," "ad audiendum iudicium," and "ad prosequendum" which we have already encountered. The qualifying phraseology indicated the purpose for which the basic habeas corpus command was issued in the first instance. I cannot believe that the

47. Anonymous, Y. B. 29 Edward III (1356), fol. xlviii (Tottel, ca. 1560).
48. Rosamond Sillem (ed.), *Records of Some Sessions of the Peace in Lincolnshire, 1360-1375* (Hereford 1936), p. lix.
49. Isobelle D. Thornley (ed.), *Year Books of Richard II, 11 Richard II, 1387-1388* (London 1937), pp. 243ff.
50. See for example: Anne Brown's Case (1497), 12 Henry VII, Keilway Rep. 3, 72 English Reports, Full Reprint 59 (hereafter cited: E. R.)
51. Jenks, "Habeas Corpus, "2 *Select Essays* 541.
52. Luke Owen Pike (ed. & trans.), *Year Books of King Edward the Third, Year XIV* (London 1888), p. 204 (hereafter cited: Pike, Year Book, 1341).
53. John de Bruer's Case, Y. B., 24 Edward III (1351), fol. xxvii (Tottel 1561).

courts were asking for the cause of detention out of idle curiosity. These early cases seem to indicate that the request for cause was generated by a claim that the commitment was unwarranted and should receive judicial attention. In short, the corpus cum causa was a writ for testing the validity of imprisonments.

On other questions relating to the appearance of the corpus cum causa, it is impossible to be so positive. Why, for example, a new form of habeas corpus was devised to meet this need can only be inferred. But bearing in mind that the court desires the production of an imprisoned party a plausible explanation can be offered. It would make no sense to issue the personal writ of subpoena to a person physically incapable of obeying it by reason of a prior commitment. Moreover, the subpoena was an original writ commencing an action, and a claim of unjust commitment presumes some legal action prior to the request for relief. The *venire facias* was a warrant for arrest for production on charges of misdemeanor and, like the capias series, issued only when the desired party was at large. Finally the writs of the liberty group were limited in use to their traditional scope. But as we have seen the basic habeas corpus command could issue to anyone having the power to execute the court's command. The habeas corpus was, in short, effective and versatile. This alone would probably recommend it to judges seeking to control commitments by inferior officials and tribunals.

A similar lack of precision must accompany any discussion as to the source of this new extension of habeas corpus. I am inclined, on slight evidence, to believe that the corpus cum causa was an invention of Chancery in the first half of the Fourteenth century. First, of the four earliest instances of the writ's use, three were from Chancery[54] and one from King's Bench.[55] Second, the corpus cum causa appears to have been adopted quite early as a regular part of Chancery process which ran as follows: (1) The petition or bill; (2) Alleging the wrong; (3) The writ—which could have been subpoena, venire facias, or corpus cum causa.[56] Certainly Chancery had a definite form for a petition which could call forth the writ of habeas corpus.[57] Finally, the corpus cum causa just happened to appear about the same time that the equitable jurisdiction of the Chancellor was taking shape. And an important part of this emerging jurisdiction was the power of discovery and

54. Y. B., 14 Edward III, *supra*, p. 18, n. 52; Y. B., 24 Edward III, *supra*, p. 18, n. 53; Milner's Case (1388) in; William Paley Baildon (ed.), *Select Cases in Chancery, 1364-1471* (London 1896), p. 9 (hereafter cited: Select Cases in Chancery).

55. John Redeswelle's Case (1356) in: Bertha Haven Putnam (ed.), *Proceedings Before the Justices of the Peace in the Fourteenth and Fifteenth Centuries, Edward III to Richard III* (London 1938), p. 59.

56. *Select Cases in Chancery*, p. xiv.

57. *Ibid.*, p. 121: ". . . . , may it please. . . your Lordship to grant a writ to have the said suppliant before you in the Chancery, together with the cause of his imprisonment."

correction of miscarriages of justice.[58] It may have been just a coincidence that the power and one of its important instruments developed about the same time. But I think that here is some slim evidence that the authority created the tool.

To summarize the findings thus far, the records show that the basic habeas corpus command of the Twelfth and Thirteenth centuries continued in use throughout the Fourteenth, and, more important, that the writ of habeas corpus sprouted a new branch called the corpus cum causa. This form, possibly an invention of Chancery, was used by that court as well as by King's Bench, and later Common Pleas, [59] to inquire into the validity of commitments. The corpus cum causa, then, was the immediate antecedent to the modern writ of liberty, habeas corpus ad subjiciendum et recipiendum. The procedural details surrounding this new form remain obscure, that is, we do not know precisely when the writ could issue, and whether claims of specific kinds of unjust commitment were necessary to justify issuance. Indeed, the records do not really indicate concretely what the court intends doing with the party although correction is implicit in the process. Most of these questions will be answered in the next century. However, one thing is clear. The connection of the writ of habeas corpus with the liberty of the subject is becoming far more proximate.

By the opening of the Fifteenth century a basic form of the writ of liberty existed. From this point on there were to be no completely new innovations of the kind indicated by the appearance of the corpus cum causa. Rather developments from 1400 were concerned with the definition and extension of the writ's scope and effectiveness. Indeed, the most notable developments of the coming ages lie not so much in the area of strict law as in the borderline region of law and politics. The corpus cum causa became a weapon of the royal courts to subdue the power of inferior and semi-independent jurisdictions. It became embroiled in the jurisdictional battles which raged within the royal court system itself. In both of these uses habeas corpus cum causa was used independently of other process, sometimes with the writ of certiorari, and very frequently with privilege.

As we have seen, by this time the habeas corpus cum causa was a regular part of Chancery process used to correct unjust judgments of inferior courts.[60] The petitioner for the chancellor's grace had to demonstrate the reason why he had been given unjust treatment in the inferior court or why he would inevitably receive such treatment and, further,

---

58. Holdsworth, *History*, Vol. I, pp. 243-45.
59. Margaret Klingelsmith (tran.) Statham's *Abridgment of the Law* (Boston 1915), Vol. 1, p. 402. Two cases appear in Stratham dated 1412 and 1431.
60. *Supra*, p. 19.

why he could not appeal to the courts of common law. If he was successful the Chancery would issue a habeas corpus, certiorari, or both, whichever course was appropriate.[61] Habeas corpus would issue if there were an indictment or pre-trial commitment involved and certiorari if proceedings in an inferior court were completed. Both might issue as one process if the court wished to assume complete jurisdiction over the matter. That is, habeas corpus was issued to produce the body and cause of commitment, while certiorari issued to remove the record of indictment or judgment.

However, I want to emphasize the fact that frequently the habeas corpus issued independently of other process. This is necessary because Professor Jenks, following Cowell's *Interpreter,* has intimated that habeas corpus during the Fifteenth century became merely a collateral assistant to certiorari.[62] Cowell, in this matter, represented an instance taken from Fitz-Herbert's *Natura Brevium* where certiorari and habeas corpus were used together as being the whole story on proper practice.[63] His version, which Jenks substantially accepts, was that a petition for certiorari was a necessary prelude to a petition for habeas corpus.[64]

Professor Jenks found further evidence for this view in the fact that by 1414 statutes aimed at correcting abuses of legal administration made possible by the use of habeas corpus and certiorari began to appear.[65] However, the "and" was not necessarily conjunctive; this statute as well as other later ones were aimed at correcting abuses possible on either certiorari or habeas corpus.[66] Except in those instances where the court wished to assume full jurisdiction, no collateral use would have been necessary. If the petitioner were at large a certiorari to review the record would be sufficient. If the petitioner were in jail the habeas corpus would bring up the body as well as that part of the record showing cause of commitment. But the correct interpretation of the usual relationship between habeas corpus and certiorari was

---

61. Francis Palgrave, *An Essay on the Original Authority of the King's Council* (London 1834), pp. 90, 134. Palgrave has an interesting petition from a John Rukke to the Chancellor. Rukke had been desseised and arrested by one John Brown. He petitioned the Chancellor to have Brown appear and answer for his wrong, to have his tenement restored, and, not least, to have himself restored to his family. The court's order read: "Coram dno Rege in canc sua, die Mart px futur videt bre de hab corpus cum causa."
62. Jenks, "Habeas Corpus, "2 *Select Essays* 539; Cf., Holdsworth, *History*, Vol. IX, pp. 108-112.
63. John Cowell, *The Interpreter* (Cambridge 1607), subtitle "Habeas Corpus"; Cf., Anthony Fitz-Herbert, *New Natura Brevium* (London, Tottel 1588), p. 250h.
64. Cowell, *op. cit.*: "Habeas Corpus is a writ, the which a man indicted of some trespass before justices of peace, or in a court of any franchise, and upon his apprehension being laid in prison for the same, may have out of the Kings Bench, thereby to remove himself thither at his own costs, and to answer the cause there. . . And the order is in this case, first to procure a (certiorari) out of the Chancery directed to the said justices for the removing of the indictment into the Kings Bench, and upon that to procure this writ to the sheriff, for the causing of his body to be brought at a day."
65. Jenks, "Habeas Corpus," 2 *Select Essays* 538.
66. 2 Henry V. st. 1, ca. 2 (1414), 2 *Stat. Realm* (1816) 176. See also: 1 Ph. & Mary, Ca. 13 (1554), 4 *Stat. Realm* (1816) 259, and 11 Henry VI (1433), 2 *Stat. Realm* (1816) 285. For judical rendering of these principles see: Robert Duplete v. Sir Gilbert Debynham (1485) in: Hemmant, *Exchequer Chamber Cases*, pp. 194-98.
67. *The Equitable Jurisdiction of the Court of Chancery* (Philadelphia 1846), Vol. I, pp. 635-687.

seen by George Spence who reported that " . . .many of these bills . . . call upon the chancellor to remove the causes to the Court of Chancery from the sheriff's court, and other inferior courts by the ancient writ of *habeas corpus cum causa*, or of *certiorari*."[67]

However, there is no question about the very intimate association of the writ of habeas corpus and the claim of privilege. Indeed, they exist side by side in the great *Abridgments* of Fifteenth and Sixteenth century law.[68] Here the habeas corpus served in an ancillary role in that action upon it was attendant upon the determination of the principal question of whether privilege would be recognized. The claim of privilege was essentially a claim that the party was subject only to certain jurisdictions or tribunals and immune from the process of all others. A man might claim the privilege of ecclesiastical courts if he were of the cloth, the privilege of Parliament if he were a member, the privilege of King's Bench if he were a clerk there or involved in an action there. The corpus cum causa served to enforce a valid claim of privilege throughout the Fifteenth, Sixteenth, and Seventeenth centuries.

As nearly as I can determine the association of corpus cum causa with privilege came about during the first years of the Fifteenth century. The first case where I find the two joined occurs in 1413,[69] a case in which the King's Bench elaborated a rule governing the privilege of that court, specifically when a claim of privilege would justify habeas corpus. The rule laid down denied the habeas corpus to a party condemned in an inferior court because, though he had previously been impleaded in King's Bench and would have normally been entitled to the privilege of that court, he had left the Bench without the judges' permission. Therefor his condemnation was good and would not be disturbed by a discharge or bail on corpus cum causa.[70] This indicates, I think, considerable practice prior to the time when actual recorded instances appear.

Whichever writ or combination of writs issued in any given case depended on the nature of the appeal and the court appealed to, but they all had the same effect. Whether habeas corpus alone or with privilege or certiorari, the effect was to curtail the authority of the inferior local and franchise jurisdictions. Throughout the Fifteenth century Common Bench interfered with London commitments by way

68. Anthony Fitz-Herbert, *La Grande Abridgement*, fol. 239 in the edition of 1516, and fol. 195 in Tottel's edition of 1577; Robert Brooks, *La Graunde Abridgement* (London, Tottel 1573 or 1586), "Privilege and Corpus cum Causa."

69. Anonymous, Y. B., 14 Henry IV, fol. 1 (London 1679, Les Reports des Cases en les Ans Des Roys Edward V, Richard III, Henry VII, and Henry VIII, Pt. 6).

70. The major rule implicit in this case of 1412 received explicit mention in a case of 1426 in: Anonymous, Y. B., 4 Henry VI, p. 8, pl. 22, Klingelsmith, *Statham's Abridgment*, Vol. I, p. 403. King's Bench ruled that if a party be impleaded in the Marshalsea he shall have a corpus cum causa to the steward, if an action be pending against him in the Bench. And if the party be condemned there, pending an action in the Bench, it shall be void and the party delivered on habeas corpus.

of habeas corpus proceedings.[71] By 1414 the practice of escaping an inferior court's commitment for debt through habeas corpus out of Chancery had become so widespread and serious that a statute of that year prohibited further releases when the return showed a commitment for debt.[72] Similarly the jurisdiction of inferior courts were constantly being determined on the combined privilege-habeas corpus process. The *Year Books* abound with references to the supervisory activity of the royal courts.[73]

The use of corpus cum causa to exert authority over the local and franchise jurisdictions which began in the early Fifteenth century was given a new twist in the latter part of the century. The habeas corpus had proven such an admirable weapon by which to protect and expand jurisdiction that it began to be used within the royal court system itself. A jurisdictional war of momumental proportions was presaged by Chief Justice Huse when he warned the Chancellor in 1483 that if the Chancery ". . .committed a suitor for breach of an injunction not to sue at common law, the court would release him by Habeas Corpus."[74] The hostility here evidenced had its root cause in the lack of distinct jurisdictional lines, the confusion and overlapping of authority characteristic of the complex Medieval court structure. It was a confusion which enabled the shrewd, litigous attorneys of the day to play off one court against another. Symptomatic of the difficulties involved was the prolific elaboration of the doctrine of privilege, just perused, whereby each court attempted to preserve the integrity of its proceedings and judgments, and perhaps extend its power as well.

The court rivalry was not confined to the relationship between Chancery and the common law courts. Indeed, the history of King's Bench, and Common Pleas from the late Fifteenth century on is largely that of a series of predatory excursions against any other tribunal which took business from them. The expanding and lucrative jurisdiction of Admiralty, for example, soon incurred the enmity of the common law courts and habeas corpus was pressed into service as an instrument to restrict the Admiral's competence. An early instance of habeas corpus from the Exchequer in 1538 might be near the beginning of the

---

71. This was particularly true when there was any claim of privilege by way of prior action in one of the Westminster courts. See: *infra.*, n. 73.
72. 2 Henry V, st. 1, ca. 2 (1414), *supra*, n. 66.
73. See for example: Anonymous, Y. B., 12 Henry IV (1411), fol. cclxvii (Trottel 1575): corpus cum caus⁃ from the Common Bench delivered a man from London arrest because an action was pending against him in the Bench: Anonymous, Y. B., 11 Henry VI (1433), fol. iv (Redman, n. d.): King's Bench delivered on corpus cum causa because party had purchased an action there and was on his way to the court; Anonymous, Y. B., 9 Edward IV (1470), fol. xxxv (Pynson, n. d.): King's Bench delivered a woman on corpus cum causa because she was on her way to the court when she was arrested on charge of debt; And see: Anonymous, Y. B., 22 Edward IV (1483), fol. xxxvi (Tottel 1578); Anonymous, Y. B., 2 Richard III III (1485), p. 16 (Les Reports des Cases, Pt. 11); Anonymous, Y. B., 14 Henry VII (1499), fol. vi (Tottel 1555); Anonymous, Y. B., 27 Henry VIII (1536), p. 20, cases 7 and 8 (Tottel 1591).
74. Y. B., 22 Edward IV, pl. 21, as cited in: Holdsworth, *History*, Vol. IX, p. 110.

attempt,[75] but certainly by 1542 we have clear evidence of a conflict in progress and the kind of weapons used. The case of *Dolphin* v. *Shutford* (1542) renders a good picture of the jurisdictional, procedural, and, indeed, constitutional problems which this inter-court conflict entailed.[76] Dolphin sued Shutford in the Court of Admiralty. Shutford, in turn, secured a writ of prohibition from the King's Bench forbidding Admiralty to proceed with the case. Along with the prohibition King's Bench issued a habeas corpus to free Shutford from the Admiral's custody. Admiralty disregarded both writs and gave judgment for Dolphin. Subsequently, Shutford instituted a suit in King's Bench against Dolphin for wrongfully suing him in Admiralty and also obtained an *alias* habeas corpus to the Admiralty Court.

The basic constitutional nature of the conflict presented in the case emerges clearly from Lord Admiral Russel's return or rather reply to the second writ of habeas corpus. The Admiral maintained that he could neither honor nor execute the writ without ". . . transgressing the law and *prejudicing the King's prerogative* and the Admiral's jurisdiction."[77] That the judges had indeed stepped on the prerogative and the Admiral's jurisdiction was demonstrated by the fact that they were called before the Council to answer for their action. And the fact that they lost this round is seen in a succinct exemplification appended to *Pyke's* case in 1553: "Habeas corpus does not run to the Admiralty Court."[78]

The common law employment of corpus cum causa against the prerogative courts is just one step away, large though it may be, from the use of the writ to question prerogative commands themselves. When this step is taken, of course, we will have the basis for the completely effective modern writ of liberty. And the taking of this step is essentially the story of late Sixteenth and Seventeenth century development. Up to this point, however, the English law had developed a reasonably effective legal instrument to protect the liberty of the subject. If the petitioner could show that he had or would receive unjust treatment at the hands of inferior courts, such as those of London, he could obtain the removal of the cause from that court or a discharge. If the inferior court had acted in excess of its jurisdiction whether absolutely or because the party was entitled to privilege, transfer, bail, or discharge could result. In short if the petitioner could justify the issuance of a writ of certorari from the Chancery, and that writ issued on almost any pretext, or if he could sustain a claim of privilege, or if he merely challenged the legal jurisdiction of the officer or court detaining him,

75. In re John Andrews (1538), in: Reginald G. Marsden (ed.), *Select Pleas in the Court of Admiralty* (London 1897), p. xiv.
76. *Ibid*, p. xlvii.
77. *Loc. cit.* (italics added).
78. *Ibid.*, p. lxxxvi.

he would have had a very good chance of obtaining habeas corpus. The changes which occurred since the Fourteenth century were mainly concerned with expanding and specifying the scope of the writ. And though this process was by no means completed, considerable progress had been made. Moreover, this progress ultimately rested upon the nature of the court system itself; it presumed a fairly coherent and orderly system for the administration of justice. It is in this broad sense, then, that the writ of habeas corpus cum causa must be viewed as an expression of the emergent equitable jurisdiction of the Chancellor as well as the centralization of judicial power in the hands of the royal courts.

CHAPTER II

The Late Sixteenth Century

Part I: Introduction

The late Tudor era is a fascinating period, a vast crucible in which strange new concoctions were brewing. Everywhere one looked the signs of radical change were in the air. A new scientific attitude challenged the rooted scholasticism as the ideas of Kepler, Galileo, Bacon and others disturbed the long sleep of creative thought. The Parliament stirred beneath a growing awareness of its power potential, while a rising merchant class reached for political authority commensurate with its economic strength. The chain reaction set off by Calvin and Luther continued to produce new and unheard of schisms, heresies, and sects. And even the arts were breaking from the feudal mold as men like Rembrandt, Shakespeare, and Corelli set world standards of excellence. Indeed, it was the sensitive artistic mind which first brooded about the trend of events. A note of confusion and sadness crept into the poet's musings as, for example, John Donne's speculation on the intellectual revolution in progress:

> The new philosophy calls all in doubt,
> The element of fire is quite put out;
> The sun is lost and the earth, and no man's wit
> Can well direct him where to look for it.
> And freely men confess that this world's spent,
> When in the planets and the firmament
> They seek so many new; they see that this
> Is crumbled out again to its atomies.

And beneath all this were the rumblings of a conflict which was to shake the very foundation of the state and restructure the constitutional principles of the commonwealth.[1]

Basically a disintegration of the Medieval commonwealth was underway. Richard Hooker's *Laws of Ecclesiastical Polity* can be viewed, in this regard, as the last great statement and rationalization of this form of social and political organization.[2] The commonwealth was not thought of in terms of royal supremacy or parliamentary supremacy, temporal or spiritual domination. Rather it conceived of an ordered

---

1. For general treatments of the currents in this period see: Basil Wiley, *The Seventeenth Century Background* (New York 1952); E. A. Burtt, *The Metaphysical Foundations of Modern Physical Science* (New York 1953); Alfred North Whitehead, *Science in the Modern World* (New York 1953), Ch. III; G. M. Trevelyan, *History of England* (New York 1953), Vol. II; S. T. Bindoff, *Tudor England* (London 1952); J. W. Gough, *Fundamental Law in English Constitutional History* (Oxford 1955).
2. See: J. W. Allen, *A History of Political Thought in the Sixteenth Century* (London 1957), Ch. VI.

polity in which all estates had their appointed role and place while each supported and aided the other in the tasks of governance. The concept of the supremacy of law, which can be traced far back into legal history, had very little operational precision, and most certainly did not imply necessarily the idea of judicial supremacy.[3] I consider Professor Sabine's characterization of Sir Edward Coke's views as a most explicit formulation of the role of law in the commonwealth:[4]

> The law assigned to every man, public or private, his rights and duties, his liberties and his obligations; it fixed the standards of justice by which he was constrained to act or forbear, and no less so if he were the king than if he were a subject. The king's rights were not the same as the subject's, but both had their rights within the law. Consequently, though the law supported innumerable powers, it knew nothing of a sovereign power, for king and parliament and the several courts of the common law had each its power indefeasible as the law provided.

This venerable and orderly system was undergoing strain in the late Sixteenth century, but it was the later claims of King James' view of the prerogative which led to the final disruption. The policy of "golden mediocritie" or common-sense compromise had kept disintegration within bounds during the late Tudor period. Nonetheless, the roots of conflict start there.

The great sea change which was beginning in this era naturally had impact on the law and the pressing interest in personal liberty and security. The interest became more articulate as men, pushing on toward new visions of social and religious life, found themselves hemmed in by the old. This is particularly manifest in the religious conflicts of the period. The Puritan sects, especially, sought to avoid the embrace of the Anglican Church and in so striving tried to invoke the assistance of the common law. Their legal strategy led to a glorification of the practically moribund Magna Carta and a use of the writ of habeas corpus. Caught in the interplay of these forces the writ became identified, in some circles at least, with the right of personal liberty.

On the strictly legal side the writ continued to be used in traditional fashions as outlined in the Fourteenth and Fifteenth centuries. Its continued and frequent use, of course, strengthened its independent position as a common law process. However, the most important development of the period was the writ's connection with executive commitments, commitments by command of the Queen or the Queen in Council. The clarification of just what was involved in this new

---

3. Gough, *op. cit.*, Ch. III.
4. George Sabine, *A History of Political Theory* (New York 1954, rev. ed.), p. 453.

development will be a major focus of attention.

It is the task of this chapter, then, to relate the unfolding of a dual character for the writ of habeas corpus—habeas corpus as the writ of liberty and habeas corpus as just another common law process but one gaining in importance. The stories will overlap, but the developments are distinct and separable. First the broad religious conflict of the period will be viewed in order to determine the role played in it by habeas corpus and to bring out the constitutional concepts with which the writ was being associated. Then the new uses of the process particularly in the area of executive commitments will be treated. Finally, as prelude to the Seventeenth century, note will be taken of the first tentative connection of these two aspects of the writ of habeas corpus.

Part 2: The Great Charter, Habeas Corpus and the Religious Conflicts of the Sixteenth Century

The religious conflicts of this period involved much more than differing interpretations of ecclesiastical organization and/or procedure. As Hooker recognized, the Puritans in refusing to conform were challenging the grounds of political authority in the Medieval Christian Commonwealth. Specifically they were denying the accepted scope of the prerogative, and while denying, asserted among other things the superior force of Magna Carta as a statement of fundamental law. Out of this turmoil the Great Charter emerged glorified as never before.

The Charter had been much neglected in the Fifteenth century and most of the Sixteenth as well. Its revival in this period can be attributed to many factors. First as Tudor rule restored order and achieved stability, a nascent English nationalism began to replace the older feudal outlook. This, in turn, encouraged a tendency to reveal and glorify the heritage of Englishmen. There is a new interest in "antiquities" and even the subject matter of the great drama is historical in tone. Magna Carta as the first great statute, the rather routinely cited beginning of statute law, partook of this revival. William Lambarde's *Archaionomia* (1568), *Eirenarcha* (1581), and the *Archeion* (1591) indicate the new interest in the English legal heritage.[5] It is significant, in this connection, that in the discussions of Magna Carta's Chapter 29 in the *Eirenarcha*, Lambarde speaks in terms of Fourteenth century interpretations of the charter. In several respects he anticipates some

---

5. The *Archaionomia* was an edition of the ancient Anglo-Saxon law which, in Holdsworth's words. ". . . restored the forgotten. . . laws to the students of the common law." The *Eirenarcha* was a treatise for justices of the peace. The *Archeion* was a short history of the common law courts and conciliar courts of Lambarde's time. It was not published until 1635.

of the notable historical errors which are usually attributed to Sir Edward Coke.[6]

By far, however, the prime factor in the revivification of the Great Charter, especially as regards Chapter 29, was its use by the Puritan wing of the Church to justify resisting attempts to enforce conformity through the instrumentality of High Commission. This tribunal originated as an administrative wing of the Privy Council for the enforcement of such statutes as the Acts of Uniformity and Supremacy. Originally separate and distinct from the regular system of ecclesiastical courts, it evolved by the 1580's into a law court asserting original and appellate jurisdiction. As long as it had remained an appendage of the Council, acting in the Council's name and resting its authority on prerogative grants of power alone, it was virtually immune from serious legal attack. The situation changed as it assumed more and more the character of an independent court:

> The whole force of any legal opposition depended entirely upon the assumption by the Commission itself of the position of a law court for the trial of suits between party and party by a definite, regular procedure in consonance with a jurisdiction which must have had some recognized limits, however broad a competence.[7]

Moreover, as it turned itself into a court with a more or less specialized jurisdiction and subject matter, the common law judges which originally participated in its proceedings ceased to be active members.[8]

In short, the High Commission rapidly became one of those "Romish" conciliar courts which the common lawyers watched with a jealous and jaundiced eye. It is due to this development that the fruitful tactical alliance of the Puritans and the common lawyers was made possible. The Puritans fought against the Commission's efforts to enforce conformity while the common lawyers hoped not only to restrict the Commission's rather elastic jurisdiction but also to curb some of its procedures which conflicted with common law notions of due process.[9]

The standard means whereby the common law courts sought to keep the eccleseiastical courts within the bounds of their proper jurisdiction was through the ancient writ of prohibition.[10] This writ, when issued, stopped all proceedings in the recipient court pending a decision

---

6. Lambarde and Coke were as one in assuming that the then current interpretations of *iudicium parium* and *per legem terrae* had held true for all time previous. See: Faith Thompson, *op. cit.*, pp. 184-187.
7. Roland B. Usher, *The Rise and Fall of High Commission* (Oxford 1913), p. 124 (hereafter cited: Usher, *Rise and Fall*).
8. *Ibid.*, p. 149.
9. Holdsworth, "The Ecclesiastical Courts and their Jurisdiction," 2 *Select Essays* 255-311, esp. at pp. 282-284; Marshal M. Knappen, *Tudor Puritanism, A Chapter in the History of Idealism* Chicago 1939\, Ch. XIII, "The Alliance with the Lawyers."
10. Ranulph de Glanville, *A Treatise on the Laws and Customs of the Kingdom of England composed in the Time of Henry II* (John Beames, trans., London 1812), Ch. XIII, p. 96ff.

by the common law court on writ of consultation as to whether the cause was lay or ecclesiastical.[11] But the writ of habeas corpus was also in evidence as a means to undermine the activities of the ecclesiastical courts. This is especially true after the establishment of High Commission. Almost on the morn of its birth Coke records an instance of habeas corpus releasing parties committed by the Commission.[12] And a clear case of a common law court questioning and determining the Commission's jurisdiction occurs in *Hinde's Case* (1576). Hinde had been committed by the Commission on charges of usury, and he was immediately released by Common Pleas on habeas corpus because the ". . .imprisonment in that case was unlawful."[13] In other words, the Common Pleas interpreted the scope of the Commission's authority and found that it could try for usury but that it could not imprison for usury. It was by such means that the common law courts finally undermined the effectiveness of the High Commission. Water, drop by drop, can eat away a mountain.

Archbishop Whitgift met the mounting opposition of the Puritan wing principally by tightening the procedures of ecclesiastical discipline. In particular he dusted off the old *ex officio* oath which, as he used it against suspected non-conformists, was a means of compulsory self-incrimination. Although the oath had good precedent behind it, the Church authorities had applied the oath sparingly in the past, and only for the most serious ecclesiastical offenses such as heresy. As was noted in connection with the background of the Fourteenth century statutes, such oaths had never been popular with the common lawyers.[14] Saint-German cited such practices as another instance of the unfavorable comparison of temporal and ecclesiastical procedure:

> An other occasion of the said dysuyon hath been by reason of dyuers sutes, yt is called in latyn, ex officio; so that the parties haue not known who hath accused them, and thereupon they haue somtyme ben caused to abiure in causes of heresies; . . . for they haue known none other accusers and that hath caused moche people in diuers partyes of this realme to thynke great malice and parcialytie in the spiritual judges . . . This is a dangerous lawe, and more lyke to cause untrewe and unlawfulle men to condempne innocentes, than to condempne offenders.[15]

---

11. Knappen, *op. cit.*, p. 270.
12. *Institutes of the Laws of England* (hereafter cited: Institutes), Part IV (London 1797), p. 333: Thomas Lee's case (1567) where Common Pleas released Lee on a habeas corpus after his commitment by the High Commission. The reason for release is not entirely clear. I suspect that it was on the basis of Lee's privilege as an attorney of the court.
13. *Loc. cit.* See also: *Ibid.*, p. 334: Thickness' case (1570).
14. *Supra,* p. 10.
15. Christopher Saint-German, *A Treatyse Concernynge the division betwene the spirytualtie and temporaltie*, fols. 16b-17b, as quoted in: Mary Hume MacGuire, "Attack of the Common Lawyers on the Oath Ex Officio as administered in the Ecclesiastical Courts in England," *Essays in History and Political Theory in Honor of Charles Howard McIlwain* (Cambridge 1948), p. 210.

However, Whitgift's strategy was to use the oath procedure vigorously in order to deprive Puritans of their livings and to involve them in fines and imprisonments. The questsions which he administered under the oath, the so-called Twenty-four articles, were in the words of the Lord Treasurer, ". . .so curiously penned, so full of branches, and circumstances as I think the Inquisitions of Spain use not so many questions to comprehend and to trap their preys."[16]

The foundation, then, of the alliance between the common lawyers and the Puritans lay in their common dislike of the High Commission and its process. The Puritans based their opposition on grounds of conscience and of common law. From their point of view it was ". . .contrarie both to the lawes of God and of the Land, to require such an oath especialle of a minister."[17] The essential weakness of the position based on conscience or the "lawes of God" was well stated in *Cartwright's Case* (1591).[18] Cartwright was hailed before the Star Chamber for refusing to take the oath *ex officio* before High Commission. His conscience did not allow him to recognize the jurisdiction of the Commission. The Attorney-General, Sir John Popham, rebutted with an ageless argument:

> Then Mr. Cartwright beginning to speak, Mr. Attourney tooke the speech from him, and made also a long speech th' effect whereof was to show how dangerous a thing yt was that men should upon the conceits of their own heads, and yet under colour of conscience, refuse the things that have been receyved for lawes of long time, and that this othe that was tendred was according to the lawes of all other lands, yet so that because they [were] the lawes of men, they carried alwayes some stayn of imperfection.[19]

Alongside their contentions of conscience, the Puritans raised objections to the Commission's procedure as not in accordance with the accepted Fourteenth century interpretations of the Great Charter. The oath *ex officio* could not be reconciled with the "fundamental law" dictates of *iudicium parium vel per legem terrae*. It was at this point that the common lawyers, especially those of Puritan persuasion, could contribute to the attack on High Commission. The lawyers raised technical questions concerning the interpretation of the Acts which the Commission was supposed to enforce, they pointed out inconsistencies in the Commission's own actions and generally made nuisances of themselves.[20]

---

16. Knappen, *op. cit.*, p. 275.
17. A. F. Scott Pearson, *Thomas Cartwright and Elizabethan Puritanism*, 1535-1603 (London 1925), app. xxiii.
18. Accounts of this case appear in: Usher, *op. cit.*, pp. 135ff; Thompson, *op. cit.*, pp. 213ff; Pearson, *op. cit.*, app. xxiii.
19. Pearson, *op. cit.*, app. xxv.
20. Knappen, *op. cit.*, Ch. XIII, *passim*.

The legal approach, however, based on the Charter was unsuccessful during this period of the 1580's and 1590's. The common law courts were not yet ready to mount a full scale attack. The courts were quite willing to snipe with prohibitions and habeas corpus, but they shied from a definitive encounter until the Seventeenth century. *Caudrey's Case* (1591) demonstrates their current determination to maintain a facade of cordial relations with the ecclesiastical structure.[21]

The competition between the common law courts and the ecclesiastical tribunals had given the Puritans hope that the former courts would come rushing to their side. The marked hesitancy of the courts to throw down the gauntlet led to a new twist in Puritan strategy. They began to concentrate their efforts in propagating their views on the meaning of the Charter possibly in the hope that this would ultimately have effect in Parliament. The fundamental law as represented in the Charter was declared to control and delimit even the royal prerogative to say nothing of the High Commission. Sir James Morice, a leading Puritan attorney, condemned the procedures of the Commission; not only were the Commission's activities ". . .injurious bothe to the Prince and people," but they were against:

> . . .the statute of Magna Carta (contayninge manie excellent lawes of the liberties and free customs of this kingdome) [where] it is ordained that no freeman bee apprehended imprisoned distrayned or impeached but by the lawe of the land. And by the statute made anno 5 E. 3. ca. 9 It is enacted that no man shal be attached uppon anie accusation contrarie to the fourme of the greate Charter & the law of the Realme. Moreover, it is accorded by the Parliament ann. 43 E. e. ca. 9 for the good government of the Cominaltie that no man bee put to answere without presentment beefor Justices, or matter of record, or by due processe, or by writte Originall after the aunciente lawe of this land. And how then shall oathes and urging this generall oathe and straighte imprisoninge of such as refuse to sweare bee justifiable?[22]

In invoking the symbolism and norms of the Great Charter, the Puritans forced the defenders of High Commission and its prerogative-based power to answer in kind.[23] Thus began the great battle of words and deeds between the advocates royal power and the protagonists of the Charter and the common law. And out of it all the procedural norms outlined in the Fourteenth century version of the Charter became irrevocably those of the common law, while Magna Carta emerged as

---

21. 5 *Coke Rep.* 1, 77 E. R. 1.
22. James Monroe, *Briefe Treatise of Oathes exacted by Ordinaries and Ecclesiastical Judges* (ca. 1592), as quoted in: Thompson, *op. cit.*, p. 220.
23. Richard Cosin, *An Apologie for Sundrie Proceedings by jurisdiction Ecclesiasticall* (London 1593), Pt. 2, Ch. 8, and Pt. III, Ch. 7.

the foundation of the right of personal liberty in the English constitution. The immense importance of this development to the progress of the writ of habeas corpus will, I think, become manifestly clear when their respective paths begin to merge.

Part 3: Common Law Developments of Habeas Corpus

Even as the Puritans were attacking the scope of the royal prerogative on claims of religious freedom unmarred by fear on the score of personal security, the common law courts were, I think, unconsciously developing a far more insidious and dangerous threat. More insidious because it was less direct and obvious. A threat more dangerous because the means and arguments were natural derivatives of a changing view of the role of the common law in the state as well as an emerging, new conception of the proper relationship between the Monarch and the Law. A strong and popular monarch might effectively stem the streams of Puritanism, but the common law rolled on like the proverbial Mississippi, characteristically either absorbing or exhausting its opponents.

We have already taken note of the common law attempts to curb the prerogative courts of Chancery, Admiralty, and High Commission by means of habeas corpus. This effort, which was extended to the Court of Requests in the late Sixteenth century,[24] continued well into the Seventeenth with varying effect on the courts involved. Between the writs of prohibition and habeas corpus the authority of High Commission was slowly being crippled, and the courts of Admiralty and Requests were restrained. Chancery was more immune due to its general control over the writ-issuing process and its power to issue the habeas corpus on its own behalf. Moreover, it had a position as a coordinate tribunal cemented by a history almost as long and prescriptive as the common law courts themselves. Most important, however, was the fact that it was closely related to the Council and was frequently headed by men of the highest ability and distinction. It will be noticed in these developments that the writ is playing an increasingly important role in conflicts which involved indirectly the royal prerogative. It is surprising indeed to find common law process challenging the authority of an action by the Court of Requests when the then current view of Requests is considered:

---

24. **Humfrey's case** (1572), Dallison 82, 123 E. R. 291. Humfrey was discharged on corpus cum causa from the Common Bench on the ground that Requests had no authority to commit for debt.

> In that the Court of *Requests* handleth *Causes*, that desireth
> *Moderation* of the *rigour* which the *Common Law* denounceth, it
> doth plainly participate with the nature of the *Chancerie*; but in
> that the *Bills* here be exhibited to the *Majestie* of the *King* onely,
> and to none other; and in that the *Masters* of *Requests* were sworne
> of the *Kings Councell*. . .[25]

This comes very near, it seems to me, to challenging the acts of the
prerogative itself by means of the habeas corpus. And we do not have
to look far for such a direct challenge or, at least, the appearance of
one. I must qualify with the phrase "or the appearance of one" simply
because I cannot be as positive as other commentators[26] as regards the
definitive interpretation of the early cases involving habeas corpus and
executive commitments.

The first such challenge by way of habeas corpus from the common
law courts occurred in the case of *Skrogges v. Coleshil* (1560)[27] which
dealt with a conflict of claims to the office of Exigenter of London. Queen
Mary had appointed Coleshil to that post and, at the same time, appointed Anthony Brown to the office of Chief Justice of Common Pleas.
When Brown assumed his post he refused to recognize Coleshil's appointment to the office of Exigenter, maintaining that the power of appointment was an incident of his office of Chief Justice. Brown then filled
the office with Skrogges, his nephew. Meanwhile Elizabeth ascended
the throne and inherited the problem.

Upon being apprized of the issue, Queen Elizabeth commanded
Sir Francis Bacon to examine the right and title of each of the contestants for the office. Bacon, in turn, called a meeting of all the judges
excepting those of Common Pleas. The judges were as one in affirming
that by ancient practice the power of appointment was an incident of
the office of Chief Justice of Common Pleas. Consequently Skrogges
was considered to be the contestant with proper title. Unsatisfied even
in the face of her judges' declaration, Elizabeth proceeded to appoint
an *ad hoc* commission to hear both contestants and her letters patent of
authority explicitly ordered the commission to confirm Coleshil if
Skrogges failed to answer before it. Moreover, if Skrogges refused to
answer before the commission, it was explicitly empowered to commit
him, presumably for contempt. Queen Mary's appointee, Coleshil, then
charged Skrogges with "deforcing" him of his rightful office whereupon
Skrogges demurred upon the bill and denied the jurisdiction of the
commission. In accordance with the letters patent of the Queen he

---

25. William Lambarde, *Archeion or, A Discourse upon the High Courts of Justice in England*, edited by Charles E. McIlwain and Paul L. Ward (Harvard 1957), p. 116.
26. Cf: Jenks, "Story of Habeas Corpus," *op. cit.*, p. 543; Holdsworth, *History*, Vol. IX, pp. 113-114.
27. 2 Dyer 175b, 73 E. R. 386-387.

was sent to jail—a commitment from which he was immediately released by habeas corpus from Common Pleas on the basis of his privilege in the Common Bench.[28]

Further difficult questions are raised by a most significant development of the latter half of the Sixteenth century, namely the recurring use of habeas corpus to bring prisoners committed by the Privy Council before the bar of the common law courts. The courts were not here dealing with an inferior or even coordinate tribunal. The Council had, since Lancastrian times, been growing in power, and Tudor policy molded it into the pre-eminent governing body of the state. It represented the various administrative and judicial facets of the royal prerogative in a far more direct and inclusive fashion than did any other state agency. The use of habeas corpus to review the actions of the Privy Council, like the writ's use in *Skrogges v. Coleshil*, appears to be a claim by the courts of common law to review and pass upon the sufficiency of cause for executive commitments. This is certainly the interpretation advanced by the common lawyers of the Seventeenth century.[29]

However, the relevant cases running from about 1531 do not really produce an answer as to whether the purview of habeas corpus and the common law courts is being extended to cover executive commitments.[30] The typical entry is singularly uninformative:

> A writ of habeas corpus ad subjiciendum et recipiendum was issued to Robert Dacres and Radulph Hopton, of the Marshalsea, commanding them to produce John Bincks before the court together with the cause of his arrest. The cause returned was that, before the receipt of the writ, Bincks had been taken and committed by command of the Privy Council on suspicion of felony and for other

---

28. *Infra*, p. 42, note 44.
29. See for example the arguments of John Selden before the House of Lords in 1628 in: 3 *Howell's State Trials* 98 *et seq.* (hereafter cited: How. St. Tr.).
30. Parker's Case, 22 Henry VIII (1531); Binck's Case, 35 Henry VIII (1544); Overton's Case, 2 & 3 Ph. and Mary (1556); Newport's Case, 4 & 5 Ph. and Mary (1558); Lawrence's Case, 9 Eliz. I (1567); Constable's Case, 9 Eliz. I (1567); Astwick's Case, 9 Eliz. I (1567); Michel's Case, 19 Eliz. I (1577); Browning's Case, 20 Eliz. I (1578); Bristow's Case, 27 Eliz. I (1585); Boyle's Case, 36 Eliz. I (1594); Harecourt's Case, 40 Eliz. I (1598). These cases are cited as supporting evidence in Glanville's Case (1615), Moore (K. B.) Rep. 838, 72 E. R. 939. Representative of the group are the following two cases: (1) Thomas Lawrence's Case (1567): Thomas Lawrence per Christopherum Draper, Mayor Civitatis Londini ac Ambrosum Nicholas et Richardum Lumbard, vicecomites ejusdem civitatis virtute brevis Dom. Reg. de habeas corpus ad prosequendum, eis inde directum. Et. coram Dom. Reg. ductus cum causa, viz: Quod septimo die November anno Reg. Dom. Eliz., Thom. Lawrence in dicto breve nominat captus fuit in divitate praedict. et in prisona dict. Dom. Reg. sub custodia praedict. vic. detent. per mandatum Concilii Dom. Reg. Qui committur Marrescallo, et postea traditur in ballium prout patet per scruet finium istius Termini. (2) Edward Newport's Case (1558): Edwardus Newport generosus per Robertum Oxenbridge mi. Constabularium Turris praedicti. virtute brevis Dom. Regis & Reginae de habeas corpus ad subjiciendum, ect., Et inde directum ad Barr. Coram Domino Rege . . . ductus cum causa, viz: quod ipse sibi commissus fruit per mandatum Consiliorum Dominae Reginae, qui committitur Marrescallo, etc., et immediate traditur in ballium, prout patet, Et postea fine die per parol, virtute brevis gestu et fama prout rotul, 17, istius anni et etiam paet super ballium inter scruet istius Termini affilat, etc.

causes that caused [political?] agitation. Immediately, by grace of the court, John Bincks committed in Great Marlow, was let to bail.[31]

We know, then, that Bincks was incarcerated on suspicion of felony by the Council, and that upon this return to a writ of habeas corpus he was bailed by King's Bench. Neither this case nor any of the others yield enough information to permit of an unequivocable statement regarding the power and function of the common law courts in these matters. The real nature of their function can only be a matter of speculation.

My feeling is that the common law courts were performing an investigatory or judicial task *for* the Privy Council. The suspicion of felony or the type of felony may not have been serious enough to warrant full scale action by the Council or the Star Chamber. In other words, *Bincks Case* may have been merely turned over to King's Bench for disposal while habeas corpus functioned as the legal instrument whereby custody and jurisdiction were transferred. It may have been, for example, that Binck's specific offense was not serious enough to warrant incarceration pending trial or he may have had sufficient surety to guarantee appearance.[32] In other cases where the prisoner was discharged altogether instead of bailed, the court may have discovered that the party imprisoned was not the party which the Council intended to have had imprisoned.[33] Such mix-ups are not uncommon even in more modern times.

What all this amounts to is a guess that the issuance of habeas corpus in these cases of executive commitments, *Skrogges* v. *Coleshil* excepted, was nothing more than a process of judicial implementation

---

31. Binck's Case, 35 Henry VIII (1544), cited in Glanville's Case, *op. cit.*, p. 939: Johannes Bincks per Robertum Dacres, Armiger Senescallus Marr. et Radulphum Hopton Marr. ejusdem curiae virtute brevis Domini Regis ad subjiciendum et recipiendum, et eis inde direct, et coram Domino Rege ductus cum causa, viz: quod ante adventum brevis praedicti Johannes Bincks captus fuit per mandatum privati Consilii Domini Regis pro suspicione felloniae et pro alliis causis illos moventibus et ductus ad Gaolem Marr. et ibidem detent virtute mandati praedicti, qui committitur. Immediate ex gratia curia special, praedictus Johannes Bincks per nomen Johannes Bincks de Magna Marlow in comitatu *Bucks weaver* traditur in ballium.

32. The finding of adequate surety seems to be the reason for bailing Richard Overton in Overton's Case, *supra*, p. 36, no. 30. William Overton and John Tayler were held responsible *corpus pro corpore*, for Richard's appearance. In parallel circumstances it was quite possible for one agency to release on a writ of habeas corpus a person arrested on process of another. However, it was customary for the discharging tribunal to assure that the discharged party would appear before the court initiating the action in the first instance. See: Carie and Denis's Case (1589), 1 Leonard (KB) 145-146, 74 E. R. 134-135. The sheriff arrested the parties on a latitat from Kings Bench. But before the return of the latitat, Chancery directed by habeas corpus that the prisoners be brought before it. There they were discharged. When Kings Bench discovered what had happened, it reprimanded the Master of the Rolls for releasing a prisoner taken on its process. The court said that ". . . it was an ill act of the Master of the Rolls: for we oftentimes have persons here upon habeas corpus who are also arrested by process out of the Exchequer, or the Common Pleas, but we will not discharge them before they have found sureties for their appearance [in the other court], and so the said courts use to do reciprocally."

33. Though not dealing with Council commitments, the following case demonstrates that this was a problem and one sometimes solved through the use of habeas corpus: Paine v. Puttenham (1572), 3 Dyer 306a, 73 E. R. 890. In this case Common Pleas criticized Chancery for sloppy procedure that resulted in the jailing of the wrong man.

of executive intentions.[34] If this be true, it might also explain the significance of the phrase *ad subjiciendum et recipiendum* which qualify the habeas corpus in *Bincks Case*. This is the first instance I have found of the full style of the modern writ being used, and it may have evolved in order to distinguish this process from others where the court ordered the production of the body. With the habeas corpus ad subjiciendum et recipiendum the court is commanding the presence of a man arrested by the Council on suspicion of felony, arrested by the highest executive process on a criminal matter. The writ was not issued as a challenge to the Council's good sense, but to give judicial effect to action initiated by the Council and to terminate the matter if possible. What action the court could take upon habeas corpus in these cases will be clarified in the discussion of *Search's Case* and *Howel's Case*.[35]

That the habeas corpus process in these instances was actually one of cooperation between the Bench and the Council is, I think, evidenced by the fact that there is no notice of conflict between the two on this score of issuing writs to bring up the Council's prisoners. It would seem reasonable to expect that if the common law courts were, in fact, challenging the power and authority of the Privy Council by way of habeas corpus proceedings there would be some record of it. This is especially true in view of the number of cases involved. As we have noted, the common law provocations of the inferior Court of Admiralty precipitated a Council meeting which ended in the temporary defeat of the Common law judges.[36] It is hardly likely that the courts could effectively challenge the parent body of the conciliar courts with impunity or without some degree of notoriety. Placed in the context of the times, it seems inconceivable indeed that the courts of common law could really challenge an Elizabethan Privy Council.

The outcome of two famous cases in 1588 buttresses the contention that the common law courts were not challenging but rather assisting executive process by means of habeas corpus. The first, *Search's Case*, was a clear and direct subversion of the Queen's commands.[37] By letters patent Queen Elizabeth had placed John Mabbe and any of his sureties

---

34. At this point only William Constable's Case (1567), *supra*, p. 36, note 30, seems to give positive evidence for this view. In an order issued to Sir John Popham, justice of Kings Bench, Queen Elizabeth commanded that the prisoners involved be let to bail in order that they might appear before the Bench for trial. Her order read as follows: "Trusty and well beloved, we greet you well. Whereas William Constable, late of London, Knight. . . for the late treasonable attempt of the late Earl of Essex, have been committed, some in one fort, some in another, and stand among others indicted of high treason for their several offenses; Forasmuch as of our princely disposition we are graciously bent to extend our grace and favor unto them, and that they shall be bailed: We command you or any of you [the judges of Kings Bench] to bail the above named persons, or any of them, to appear before us in our court commonly called Kings Bench, at such time, and in such manner and form as to you, or any of you, shall seem meet. And this shall be your sufficient warrant and discharge in that behalf?"
35. *Infra*, pp. 38ff.
36. *Supra*, p 23ff.
37. 1 Leonard (KB) 70, 74 E. R. 65-66.

under her protection specifying that if any person arrest Mabbe or any of his sureties, then that person arresting or causing the arrest was to be himself arrested by the Marshal of the House and held until he answered for his contempt before the Council. William Search caused one of Mabbe's sureties to be arrested, and was therefor himself arrested by the Marshal of the House.

The next act opens with Search petitioning the Court of Common Pleas to deliver him from the custody of the Marshal by a writ of habeas corpus. The writ issued, and the Marshal returned that Search was arrested and held in custody on the authority of letters patent of the Queen, citing the relevant portions. Evidently the court considered this an insufficient return and Search was discharged from custody, whereupon he was arrested again by the Marshal on the same grounds as before. Common Pleas answered this contempt of its process with an attachment against the Marshal. Like *Skrogges* v. *Coleshil* before it, there is no way of viewing this case as other than a direct flaunting of the highest executive command. Inferentially, Search's discharge meant that the court considered either that the Marshal had no power to arrest and commit even on the basis of the Queen's explicit command or that the Queen herself did not possess such power except as exercised through normal common law process.

Common Pleas must have been in an obstreperous humor during the Michaelmas term of 1588 for following hard on the heels of *Search's Case* the court frustrated the process of the Privy Council in *Howel's Case.*[38] For reasons unknown Howel had been committed to the Marshalsea by order of Lord Chancellor Francis Walsingham. The Court of Common Pleas issued a habeas corpus to the Marshal of the Marshalsea who returned that Howel was in his custody ". . .per mandatum Francisci Walsingham Militis Principalis Secretarij, and unius de privato concilio dominae reginae." Common Pleas held this return to be insufficient and allowed time for the Marshal to amend his return. On the second time around the Marshal returned that Howel had been committed by order of the entire Privy Council. And this also the court held insufficient for ". . .by whatsoever person, or by what means soever he was committed. . ." did not show.

Whatever the intentions of Common Pleas had been in these cases, there is no question about how the Privy Council interpreted them. The Council's reaction indicates strongly that Common Pleas' action in these cases was not only unprecedented but presumptious as well. And in order to ensure that such situations would not recur, the judges were compelled to place on record the prevailing conceptions of

38. I Leonard (KB) 70, 74 E. R. 65-66.

proper practice on the writ of habeas corpus. Their collective opinion is recorded in the *Resolution of the Judges* of 1592:

> And where it pleased your Lordships, to will divers of us to set down in what cases a person sent to custody by her Majesty, her Council, some one or two of them, are to be detained in prison and not delivered by her Majesties Courts or Judges. We think that if any person be committed by her Majesties commandment from her person, or by order from the Council-board, or if any one or two of her Council commit one for high treason such persons so in the case before committed may not be delivered by any of her Courts without due tryal by the Law and Judgement of acquital had.[39]

With the Resolution in mind, the significance of *Search's* and *Howel's Cases* along with those which preceded them is somewhat clarified. The Council did not object to habeas corpus proceedings in the traditional manner, that is proceedings which were confined to questions other than the ultimate validity of executive commitment itself. Nor did the government demand that the question of validity of commitment be altogether exempted from the judicial process, but only that this centrally important issue be tested in full trial proceedings and not in a summary manner as on the return to the writ.

Without, perhaps, being fully conscious of the political implications of their action, the judges of Common Pleas had attempted to expand the effectiveness of habeas corpus process as regards executive commitments as they had already expanded it in other areas. But the time was not ripe for the establishment of a judicial check on executive action. They were compelled to reaffirm past practice, namely, that they would not release prisoners of the Council until "due tryal by the Law and Judgment of acquital" was had. In practice this meant that those held by executive command, when held *per speciale mandatum,* would be remitted after the return to the writ of habeas corpus had been heard. The form of the remittitur was not that of a final judgment and meant, in effect, that the judges would hold under advisement the question as to whether the prisoner should be delivered until a trial established guilt or innocence. From the standpoint of the protection of personal liberty, the *Resolution* meant that if the Monarch or his Council refused to specify the particular cause of imprisonment and refused to bring the cause to trial, then the prisoner had no legal means to force the situation and secure a resolution by process at the common law.

I cannot construe this episode as a great judicial revolt in the cause of personal liberty. The step taken by Common Pleas was a natural

---

39. I Anderson's Rep. 297, as reprinted in: Holdsworth, *History*, Vol. V, app. I, p. 495.

one in the development of the writ of habeas corpus. Exchequer, Admiralty, High Commission, the Sheriff of London, and so forth had had to submit to habeas corpus process, submit cause, and suffer their prisoners discharged on grounds of insufficiency or lack of jurisdiction. Why not then prisoners of executive commitments? The judges' complaints, also embodied in the *Resolution,* suggest that they were motivated by the frustrating obstacles and impediments which their process encountered when executive commitments were involved. And these complaints provide a valuable insight into the difficulties facing an imprisoned person even in this relatively advanced stage of legal development.

The judges charged that ". . .divers have been imprisoned for suing ordinary Actions and Sutes at the common Law until they have been constrained to leave the same against their wills."[40] Moreover, prisoners had been committed in "secret places" so that the judges of the common law cannot learn to whom to direct her Majesties Writs, and by this means Justice cannot be done."[41] Even officers of the court had been arrested for attempting to discharge the orders of ". . .her Majesties Court at Westminster, and thereby her Majesties Subjects and Officers so terrified, as they dare not sue or execute her Majesties Laws, her Writs, and Commandments."[42] Most important, the judges treated the writ of habeas corpus as if it were a remedy which existed as of right for all prisoners. For even though they admitted the validity of Council commitments *per speciale mandatum* and their inability to discharge on such a return, they nonetheless insisted that:

> . . .the Judges may award the Queen's Writs to bring the bodies of such persons before them, and if upon return thereof the causes of their commitment be certified to the Judges as it ought to be, then the Judges in the Cases before ought not to deliver him, but to remand the prisoner to the place from which he came.
> Which cannot conveniently be done unless notice of the cause in generality or else specifically be given to the Keeper or Gaoler that shall have custody of such prisoner.[43]

It is this "complaining" section of the Resolution rather than the capitulation itself that constitutes the longrun significance and importance of this entire matter.

For even while admitting to their powerlessness in the face of executive commitments, the judges doggedly insisted on their right to issue the writ in any case of commitment. Moreover, in their capitulation

---

40. I Anderson's Rep., in Holdsworth, *History,* Vol. V, app. 1, p. 495.
41. *Loc. cit.*
42. *Loc. cit.*
43. *Loc. cit.*

the judges publicized the shortcoming of the current legal protection of the right of personal liberty as well as the fact that the writ of habeas corpus was the best, if imperfect, instrument to provide the subject with some measure of security. The Parliamentary-Common Law faction of the Seventeenth century will felicitously misconstrue these Sixteenth century practices in their battle against arbitrary and unchecked executive commitments. So often progress is legitimized by a misconstruction of the past.

I have emphasized in this section the emerging connection of the writ of habeas corpus with commitments by high executive process because I feel that this was the most interesting and significant development of the period. But I would not want to give the impression, by omission, that the uses and developments of the preceding period became obsolete. The ancillary connection of habeas corpus and privilege continued to be important and extensively used. Indeed, the ultimate rationale of the court's release of Skrogges in the case of *Skrogges* v. *Coleshil* discussed previously was the fact that he was entitled to the privilege of the Common Bench "...because he was a necessary minister to the Court."[44] By 1570 every officer of Common Bench, Exchequer, King's Bench and Chancery had been immunized against the process of inferior courts such as those of London. If such officers were sued and/or committed in inferior tribunals they were automatically entitled to writs of privilege and habeas corpus.[45] The central courts at Westminster continued also to determine the customs or jurisdiction of inferior courts on the writ of habeas corpus. For example in 1599 King's Bench ruled that the customs of London did not confer jurisdiction to hear cases of slander, and the petitioner was not remanded.[46]

Before turning to the Seventeenth century one word of explanation is needed. Strictly speaking we now have two forms of the corpus cum causa, the original inheritance and the *ad subjiciendum* branch. This latter form appears in relation to criminal commitment by king and Council, but it is impossible to say whether this form was concerned exclusively with criminal commitments. More often than not, the court records—even the *Resolution of the Judges*—make no distinction as to form, and it is probable that no clear distinction was made since they could both serve the same fundamental purpose. Not until criminal commitments by the Council became frequent and enmeshed in political controversy were these two forms clearly separated, the original becoming exclusively associated with commitments stemming from non-criminal matters while the *ad subjiciendum* form becoming strictly used in

---

44. 2 Dyer 175a, b, 73 E. R. 386.
45. See: William Hughes, *The Grand Abridgment of the Law* (London 1660), Vol. I, p. 473.
46. Oxford and Ux v. Cross (1599), 4 Cook 18a, 76 E. R. 902.

criminal commitments. If it were known when Edward Coke composed the relevant passages in the *Second Institutes,* where the two are separated, it would help establish approximately when the two forms began being clearly distinguished.[47] The best I can do is advance the fact that by 1627, the year of *Darnel's Case,* a clear distinction was being made,[48] and from that time forward all writs concerned with criminal commitments were of the *ad subjiciendum* variety while all others used to test the validity of commitments were of the older form, a form distinguished then by the phrase *ad faciendum et recipiendum.* Actually the slow separation of these two forms caused no problems in the period to which I want to give major attention. However, toward the mid-Seventeenth century all manner of technical difficulties arose due to the separation and the complete obscurity of practice during the late Sixteenth and early Seventeenth centuries.[49]

Part 4: Prelude to the Seventeenth Century

As we have seen, the Puritan strategy in the struggle with High Commission led to an exhaltation of the Great Charter and a use of habeas corpus to subvert the authority of the ecclesiastical courts. When they spoke of the Charter they meant, of course, the Fourteenth century version of it. In particular they revived the old objections to the use of *ex officio* oath procedure and the initiating of action by information. In both instances the underlying complaint, as far as legal procedure was concerned, was the ability of the Commission to start and terminate proceedings in a very private manner. There were no open court hearings, no notifications of cause, and no formal means of appealing judgments. Judging from the protection of defendant's rights accorded by the common law, I do not think that the Puritans could claim that ecclesiastical trials were less fair. But certainly ecclesiastical proceedings could not be as easily frustrated on technical points of procedure. Ecclesiastical procedure was, then, in some respects more effective. And this was the real complaint though it was stated in terms of a violation of proper due process.

A similar complaint was registered by the judges as regards Council action. The Council could detain a man indefinitely without notifying anyone of the cause. It could remove the party out of reach of the King's writs and, in other ways, frustrate the normal course of judicial proceedings. Thus the abortive but natural attempt to expand the scope of the writ's competence and, of course, the issuing court's authority. The general move constantly to expand authority partly through the

47. *Institutes,* Part II (London 1671, 4th. ed.), pp. 52-53.
48. *Infra,* pp. 59ff.
49. *Infra,* pp. 80ff.

use of habeas corpus, as we have seen, had been in progress since at least the beginning of the Fifteenth century. I cannot see this move as a noble gesture on behalf of the cause of personal liberty or as a direct attack on the prerogative as was the case in some Puritan thought. However, the result would have been the same had both movements succeeded. To define an area of religious freedom or to bring executive commitment under court control would have meant a substantial confinement of prerogative power. And to effect both of these purposes the writ of habeas corpus was shown to be a tool of considerable potential.

The possibilities of an alliance between the due process standards of the Great Charter and the instrumental virtues of habeas corpus as a possible means to effect both of the above purposes did not go unnoticed. It is almost symbolic that the first concrete proposal along these lines came from James Morice, prominent Puritan and prominent common lawyer. In 1593 he introduced in the House of Commons a bill for *Confirminge a branche of Magna Carta* demonstrating the connection between the two movements and the possible result of the relationship admirably:

> Whereas the bodies of sundrie of her Majesties subjects without anie suite, or Lawful proces or Arrest or without sufficient warrant or ordinary and due course and proceedinge in Law, onlie uppon some sinister and unjust accusation or information and by the procurement of some ambitious persons have bene committed to prison and ther remaine to their grevous and intollerable vexacion and contrary to the great Charter and auncient good Lawes and statutes of this realme.
>
> Fore remedy whereof be it enacted: That the provisions and prohibicions of the said great Charter and other Lawes in that behalfe made be dulie and inviolatelie observed. And that no person or persons be hereafter committed to prison but yt be by sufficient warrant and Authorities and by due course and proceedings in Lawe uppon paine that he or thei that shall so procur anie person to be committed or imprisoned contrarie to the Lawes aforesaid and the true meaning of this Act shall forfeite to the partie so imprisoned his treble damages systeyned by reasons of anie suche imprisonment...
>
> And that the Justice of anie the Queenes Majesties Courts of Recorde at the common Lawe maie awarde a writt of habeas Corpus for the deliverye of anye person so imprisoned and yf the keeper of the prison or his deputie shall after notice of such writt deteyne the bodie of such person so committed he shal forfeit and loose to the partie so greaved [L 40] of Lawfull englishe money and shall also answear to the said partie Treble damages. . .[50]

50. *Harleian Manuscript,* 6847, fols. 64-65, as quoted in: Thompson, *op. cit.,* app. G, p. 394.

Morice's bill never became law. The Speaker of the House, ironically Sir Edward Coke, shelved the bill and it died from the Queen's displeasure. But as we shall see in the course of the Seventeenth century, a very hardy seed had been planted.

CHAPTER III

The Constitutional Conflicts of the Seventeenth Century and the Emergence of the Writ of Liberty

Part 1: The Normative Perfection of Habeas Corpus as the Writ of Liberty

Introduction

The problems which plagued the reigns of the first Stuart kings had their roots, as we have already noted, in the Tudor period. Nonetheless they operated in a substantially different context. The penetration of the mists of English constitutional and legal history went deeper as law men such as Edward Coke, John Selden, and Henry Spelman laid bare what they believed to be the constitutional heritage of Englishmen.[1] Probing and debate were no longer seriously curtailed by the threat of imminent invasion and the consequent emphasizing of executive, prerogative power which that condition entailed. Spain and Ireland ceased to be important dangers, the United Provinces were friendly, and Scotland was dynastically united with England. With these problems in the background, constitutional issues could and did move to the forefront of men's minds.[2]

Religious problems also had taken a new turn. At the beginning of Elizabeth's reign the triumph of Protestantism and the reform of the Church Universal had seemed almost assured of success. Throughout the later Sixteenth century, however, the counter-reformation gained momentum. Learning the uses of adversity, the Roman Church emerged again as a dynamic force while the progress of Protestantism was not only halted but pushed back. "The temper of every earnest Protestant," in John Green's characterization, "was that of a man who, after cherishing the hope of a crowning victory is forced to look on at a crushing and irremediable defeat."[3] This situation conduced to the spread of intolerance and dogmatism. The kind of appeal which Hooker had made to

---

1. Holdsworth, *History*, Vol. V, Ch. 5, "The literature of the common law."
2. J. R. Tanner, *English Constitutional Conflicts of the Seventeenth Century*, 1603-1689 (Cambridge 1928), p. 5.
3. John Richard Green, *A Short History of the English People* (New York 1900, rev. ed.), Vol. II, p. 158.

reasonableness on form while adhering to substantive truth in doctrine could not succeed in an atmosphere permeated by mistrust, a milieu in which every trivial difference became a matter for bitter debate and acrimonious charges of un-Godliness. The resulting intensification of religious problems added to otherwise dry legal and constitutional debates a moral passion which inflamed and expanded the scope of conflict.

But perhaps the most important difference between the Tudor and Stuart periods lay in the personalities and attitudes of the Stuart kings themselves. The subjects of "good Queene Bess" were vastly relieved to have avoided a disputed succession, to have obtained a solid Protestant, and a man whose scattering of honors and favors on the road from Edinburgh presaged a generous monarch. Only slightly was their welcome tempered by a most prescient caution:

> Thou wilt not alter the foundation
> Thy ancestors have laide of this estate,
> Nor grieve thy Land with innovation,
> Nor take from us more than thou wilt collate.[4]

But James I lacked the tact in handling subjects and the fierce pride in English institutions which was the source of Elizabeth's great sway over her people. The new king was not an innovator, at least in his own mind, nor was he the "slobbering pedant" sometimes charged.[5] But he did have an unquestioned ability to say and do the wrong thing at the wrong time. The political theory expressed in his *Trew Law of Free Monarchies* was not calculated to appeal to a proud Parliament and people. Elizabeth once told the members of Commons that the glory of her crown resided in the fact that she ruled with their love; all present fell prostrate with gratitude. James, in turn, relegated the entire Parliament to the position of "head Court of the King" whose subordination to the Monarch was shown by the fact that although the king may make law without Parliament, Parliament cannot make law unless the king's "Scepter be to it, for giving it the force of a law."[6] It may have been true, but few appreciated such a blunt statement.

James was never to witness the full fury of the storm he did so much to exorcise; "...although he had a genius for getting into difficulties, he was not without a certain shrewdness in stopping just short of catastrophe. If he steered the ship straight for the rocks, he left his

---

4. Samuel Daniel, A Panegyric Congratulatory delivered to the King's Most Excellent Majesty (1603), stanza 30, as quoted in: Gough, *op. cit.*, p. 51.

5. Maurice Ashley, *England in the Seventeenth Century* (London 1948), p. 41.

6. *The Trew Law of Free Monarchies*, in: Charles H. McIlwain (ed.), *The Political Works of James I* (Cambridge 1918), p. 62.

son to wreck it."[7] And Charles I proceeded to do just that. He opened his reign on a note of religious conflict, and ended it with a civil war which claimed his annointed head. Charles immediately antagonized the increasingly Puritan Protestantism of his realm by backing the Laudian Reaction which proved so beneficial to the colonization of American shores. Adding insult to injury, he married a Catholic princess at a time when all England feared the consequences of two religions lying in the same bed. To complete the picture, he deftly managed to anger both houses of Parliament by "trenching on their ancient liberties" and shamed the nation with a foreign policy composed of a long series of expensive and humilating fiascoes.[8]

It was against this dark backdrop that the habeas corpus emerged definitively as the writ of liberty. It would be a mistake to search for any radically new developments in the process. As we have seen, the seed for this growth had already been planted by the end of the Sixteenth century. Rather the key to understanding Seventeenth century developments lies in a recognition of a new tempo of change, and new intensity of strife. Constitutional issues quietly implicit in several previous developments suddenly acquire explicitness and hosts of protagonists to debate them. The direction in which the habeas corpus moved in the earlier period was not changed, but like all else its movement was vastly accelerated. Not only was the writ used more frequently against the rivals of the common law courts, but the political implications of its use as a means to test validity of all commitments began to be fully appreciated. Kings as well as common lawyers began to understand habeas corpus, as some wanted to develop it, would become more than just another common law process, but legal process capable of paring the prerogative.

In the first part of this Chapter, I want to carry the development of habeas corpus to the Petition of Right. The Petition, I think, marked the end of the normative development of the writ. Tha is, by this time men knew what they wanted from the process or what they wanted to avoid. The issues were clearly drawn, and the implications of a fully effective habeas corpus applicable both to criminal and non-criminal commitments were obvious to all contenders. For convenience's sake I will treat first of the developments arising out of the full scale attack launched by the common law courts on the ecclesiastical structure, the conciliar courts, and the local jurisdictions. Then I will turn to the effort to establish a judicial check upon executive commitments. This later topic falls naturally into two phases. First there was the attempt to persuade the King's Bench to take the initiative, and then the

---

7. H. M. Gwatkin, *Church and State to the Death of Queen Anne*, p. 276, as cited in: Tanner, *op. cit.*, p. 51.
8. Trevelyan, *op. cit.*, Vol. II, pp. 163-165.

Parliament entered with its proposals culminating in the Petition of Right.

Habeas Corpus and the Jurisdictional Conflicts of the Seventeenth Century

One of the most marked features of Seventeenth century legal life was the rapacious posture of the common law courts. Greedy for jurisdiction and seized of the notion that they represented the paramount law administering agencies of the state, these courts never tired of restricting the activities of other tribunals whenever and wherever possible. The beginnings of this battle for supremacy in an earlier period has already been noted; in this era only the intensity not the direction of events is changed.

As part of this intensified development there was an increased use of habeas corpus by the common law courts. The courts had other means such as the writ of prohibition to restrict competitors, but given habeas corpus it is obvious why it should have been eagerly employed. What better way to undermine the jurisdiction and effectiveness of rival tribunals than to destroy the efficacy of their sanctions? No man would tremble before High Commission, for example, if he knew that a habeas corpus from King's Bench or Common Pleas could vitiate the Commission's order of commitment.

Conflict with the ecclesiastical courts.—The High Commission emerged from the Hampton Court Conference of 1604 with its jurisdiction and authority undiminished over the strong protests of Puritan elements. Moreover, it was considerably reinforced in its efforts to secure conformity by King James' undisguised hatred of the presbyterian form of Protestantism as well as his personal defense of *ex officio* oath procedure. The zeal with which James' High Commission set to work is shown in the fact that in a short while some three hundred clergymen had been deprived of their offices for refusing to subscribe *ex animo to* the Canons of 1604. This increased activity of the Commission and the ecclesiestical courts in general served to exacerbate the relations between the ecclesiastical structure and the common law courts. Additionally, of course, it spurred the Puritans to increase their opposition by all means available.

The common law courts, for their part, continued chewing away at the authority of the Commission and its subordinate tribunals in the ecclesiastical court system. They refused to allow the Commission to commit for nonpayment of alimony,[9] to have any jurisdiction over ordinary felonies, that is, not within the classification of "heinous"

---

9. Sir Anthony Roper's Case (1608), 12 Coke Rep. 45-48, 77 E. R. 1326-1328; Agar's Case (1611), 2 Brownlow and Goldesborough 36, 123 E. R. 801; Bradstone v. the High Commission Court (1615), 2 Bulstrode 301, 80 E. R. 1138.

ecclesiastical offenses such as heresy,[10] or to exercise any jurisdiction whatever over persons entitled to the privilege of the common law courts.[11] In short, the common law judges resolved that they had full authority to define and delimit the jurisdiction of the High Commission.[12] And if the Commission acted in excess of the jurisdiction so defined and commitment resulted, the party would be released on habeas corpus.

There was little question but what the common law courts were primarily interested in eradicating the judicial competence of High Commission altogether, and failing that to restrict it as narrowly as possible. As before, the hostility of the common lawyers stemmed from the continued and extensive use of *ex officio* oath procedure in the ecclesiastical courts. Opponents of the High Commission were quite aware that if they were able to bring the procedure into disrepute they would, in effect, destroy the Commission's effectiveness. For without such procedure heresy would be immensely difficult to establish and excommunication impossible to justify.[13] The common law courts objected to the procedure on *ex officio* oath because it dispensed with the regular indictment and trial of the common law and because the party to whom the oath was administered was given no indication of the charges against him.[14] It was upon these themes that the Commission's enemies constantly played.

The Puritans being the group most immediately affected by the Commission's activities were, of course, the most interested in finding common law devices by which to undermine the Commission's effectiveness. I have noted in connection with Sixteenth century developments the first tentative moves toward an alliance with the common lawyers and the reason for a convergence of interest between the two groups. That the Puritans did not allow their limited Sixteenth century success to discourage further efforts was shown by the fact that from 1604 instructions circulated in Puritan circles advised those caught in the clutches of High Commission to seek writs of habeas corpus or prohibition from the common law courts.[15] This in itself is an index to the growing efficacy of the process and the willingness of the courts to interfere.

The Puritans also continued their efforts to bring about an identification of Magna Carta due process arguments and the writ of

---

10. Roy v. Dighton (1616), 1 Rolle 220, 81 E. R. 445; Dighton v. Holt (1616), 1 Rolle 337, 81 E. R. 527; Codde's Case (1616), 1 Rolle 245, 432, 31 E. R. 468, 588.

11. Case note (1609), 2 Brownl. & Goldes, 270, 123 E. R. 937.

12. *Loc. cit.*

13. Usher, *Rise and Fall*, p. 182.

14. For example, the absence of these conditions was the reason given by King's Bench for the bailing of one John Burrowes: John Burrowes, William Cox, et al. against the High Commission Court (1616), 3 Bulstrode 49-55, 31 E. R. 42-47.

15. Roland B. Usher, *The Reconstruction of the English Church* (New York 1910), Vol. II, pp. 362-365.

habeas corpus in the general effort to strengthen the hand of the common law courts in their dealings with High Commission. The spirit of Morice's bill did not die when Coke shelved it. *Nicholas Fuller's Case* (1607) is a perfect example of these continuing efforts.[16] Fuller, an attorney before King's Bench, was retained as counsel for some gentlemen arraigned before the High Commission and subsequently committed by that tribunal. He immediately petitioned King's Bench for a writ of habeas corpus to free his clients alleging as reason for issuance that the Commission had exceded its rightful jurisdiction and had committed without due process. He assailed the legality of the oath procedure which had ensnared his clients and charged that, in effect, men were jailed at the absolute discretion of the Commissioners and kept ". . .in jail as longe as they list."[17] This was all contrary to the dictates of the Great Charter, and habeas corpus should *therefor* issue.

Ironically Fuller himself prevented the King's Bench from utilizing this ready-made test case. His zeal led him to become far too vitriolic in his attack on High Commission. The immediate result was his arraignment before the Commissioners on a charge of slanderous impeachment of the royal prerogative in causes ecclesiastical.[18] King's Bench then issued a writ of prohibition staying the proceedings in High Commission against Fuller. Subsequently however, the Bench admitted the jurisdiction and withdrew its prohibition. Believing that it would be nettled no further, the Commission fined and committed the over-zealous Fuller only to discover, however, that its warrant of commitment was challenged by a habeas corpus from King's Bench to release the prisoner. In view of King's Bench previous admission of jurisdiction, there was no possible way to justify the habeas corpus.[19]

This last development brought King James into the fray, and the matter changed from a dispute between courts to an issue of state importance. James recognized that Fuller could not well contend, in the face of the judges' concession, that the Commission had no jurisdiction to try him. Rather the arguments on the return to the last issued habeas corpus would have to focus on whether it was within the scope of the royal prerogative to grant powers of fining and commitment to the Commission in cases not involving heresy. And the king would have no court of common law or any other attempting to define the royal prerogative. The weight of his majesty confined the arguments on the return very narrowly, and Fuller was ultimately remanded to the custody of the

---

16. A rather sketchy version of the case appears in 12 Coke Rep. 41-45, 77 E. R. 1322-1325. My treatment is based upon the manuscript-based analysis of Prof. Usher: Usher, *Rise and Fall*, pp. 170-179.

17. Usher, *Rise and Fall*, p. 173.

18. *Loc. cit.*

19. *Ibid.*, at p. 177.

Commission.[20]

I think these cases arising out of the hostility between the common law and ecclesiastical courts demonstrate nicely the free-swinging use of habeas corpus characteristic of this period. It is quite obvious that the common law judges regarded it as a most efficacious process, and it is equally clear that the Puritans regarded the writ as the best guarantee of their liberty. However, most important is the evidence of a continuing effort to forge a bond between the Great Charter of English Liberties and the writ of habeas corpus.

Conflict with the conciliar courts.—As I indicated in the previous chapter, the common lawyers' objections to the conciliar courts were based, as far as the law was concerned, on much the same grounds as their hostility to the ecclesiastical courts. In addition, and on a more materialistic level, the courts of common law looked with undisguised envy on the very lucrative practice enjoyed by some of these tribunals.[21] It is not surprising then to witness a continuing attack on their authority.

The persistance of the common law courts is admirably demonstrated by the renewed, and this time successful, effort to extend the authority of habeas corpus to the Court of Admiralty. As will be recalled, the exemplification of 1553 specifically banned such an extension.[22] However, by 1605 Common Pleas was bailing Admiralty prisoners on the ground that the Admiral's returns to the court's habeas corpus were insufficient in that they were not precise enough concerning the cause of commitment to enable the Common Pleas to judge whether the Admiral was acting within his proper sphere of jurisdiction.[23] Similarly the Court of Requests continued to enjoy the surveillance of the common law courts through habeas corpus.[24]

The common law courts also entered the field against the various regional administrative wings of the Council, such as the Councils of Wales and York.[25] These minor councils were particularly offensive to the courts as they were considered to be mere administrative usurpers of judicial functions. Writs of prohibition and habeas corpus inundated the area of authority held by these councils. By 1629 the government was desperately casting about for means to protect them in the exercise of their delegated functions. But in a meeting called to provide a solution, Coke vigorously defended the common law courts in their obstructionist activity. If, as he argued, the number of writs from the

---

20. Usher, *Rise and Fall*, p. 177.
21. Rachel Robertson Reid, *The King's Council in the North* (London 1921), Ch. VI, *passim.*
22. *Supra*, p. 24.
23. Thomlinson's Case (1605), 12 Coke Rep. 104, 77 E. R. 1379; *accord*, Hawkeridge's Case (1616), 12 Coke Rep. 129, 77 E. R. 1404.
24. Sir Henry Lea's Case (1613), Godbolt 199, 78 E. R. 120.
25. For the use of writs of prohibition in these cases see: Knightley D'Anvers, *A General Abridgment of the Common Law*, (London 1705-1713), Vol. 1, p. 676, pl. 13.

common law courts had increased in recent times it was not due to any imagined hostility or jealousy, but rather to the vastly increased activity of the Councils themselves.[26]

Habeas corpus also continued to serve as a check on Chancery interference with common law process. This, of course, goes back to 1483[27] and sometimes the writ was effective, sometimes not. In *Addis' Case* (1609), for example, habeas corpus encountered the personal interest of the king and the judges backed down.[28] Addis, being party to a suit in King's Bench, was travelling to London for an appearance at court. On his way he was arrested and held on warrant from the Lord Chancellor. King's Bench usually maintained that when anyone was involved in the business of the court he was entitled to the court's privilege until the matter was terminated. Consequently, the Bench issued a habeas corpus to obtain Addis, but the return stated that Addis was being held on matters concerning the king and for that reason he could not be produced. The Bench thought this return much too general, but being unsure as to the proper course of action, it took the matter under advisement.

Glanville's Case (1615) offered a somewhat different problem.[29] First, the direct interest of the king was not present to limit the judge's freedom of action. Second, the case involved the much more serious matter of direct interference with the execution of common law judgment. Glanville had been committed by Chancery for ignoring an injunction not to execute a judgment he had obtained from King's Bench. King's Bench immediately discharged him from that commitment on the ground that once judgment had been given at the common law only Parliament, not Chancery, could reverse or block it. That Chancery was not overly impressed with this argument is shown by the fact that it immediately re-committed Glanville. Whereupon, Justice Coke of King's Bench issued another habeas corpus citing precedents going back to 1567 as authority for King's Bench's power to release prisoners of Chancery on habeas corpus. Unless Coke had more information on these past cases than I was able to locate, I fear they did not support him very well.[30]

In the first place, the Sixteenth century cases Coke adduced do not, at least on their face, deal with commitments by the Chancery. In the

---

26. The Case of the Lords Presidents of Wales and York (1629), 12 Coke Rep. 50, 77 E. R. 1331. In his argument Coke adduced many precedents to justify the action of the common law courts, and referred to a "book of Habeas Corpus" which specifically justified the use of habeas corpus in such cases. I have never encountered any other reference to that book, or even an intimation that such a manual existed.
27. *Supra*, p. 23.
28. Croke, Jacobi 219, 79 E. R. 190.
29. Moore (K. B.) Rep. 838, 72 E. R. 939. Involving the same kinds of issues were: Glandfield's and Courtney's cases (1615), 1 Rolle 111, 81 E. R. 365; Doctor Googe's and Smith's cases (1616), 1 Rolle 278, 81 E. R. 487.
30. *Supra*, p. 36, no. 30.

second place, the current cases indicated that proper practice was not entirely clear. Three cases in the year following *Glanville's Case* pretty well demonstrate this. In the first, King's Bench discharged a petitioner on habeas corpus from Chancery commitment when the return showed only a charge of contempt.[31] In the next case, the prisoner was remanded when the return showed that the party had been committed for not obeying a decree of Chancery.[32] In the last case the return again showed commitment for contempt of Chancery. But the return was subsequently amended to specify the reasons why the party was judged in contempt. On this amended return, the King's Bench doubted that it knew the proper course to take, so the judges did nothing—that is, they took the matter under advisement.[33] And at this point, no generalization as to what constituted proper practice as between Chancery and the common law courts can be made.

As was the case with the ecclesiastical courts, these instances of the use of habeas corpus against the conciliar courts demonstrate the extensive and sometimes devastating jurisdictional purposes to which the process was being addressed. The due process aspect of the writ's development was more obvious in the use of habeas corpus against the ecclesiastical courts largely because of deliberate Puritan tactics. In the use of the writ against the conciliar courts this aspect remained, for the time being, largely implicit in the basic motivation of the common law attack.

Supervision of local and special authorities.—The jurisdictional aspect of the heated rivalry between the conciliar and common law courts was sufficient to mask the basic and underlying difference on what constituted proper indictment and trial procedure. However, this was not the case in the relation between the common law courts and the minor jurisdictions. In this area the supremacy and supervisory power of the common law courts had long been established. Consequently the basic procedural norms which these courts sought to establish and maintain were more explicit.

In the *Case of the Marshalsea* (1613), for example, King's Bench overturned a judgment rendered by the Court of the Steward and Marshal on the ground that it conflicted with the requirements of Magna Carta and due process.[34] Specifically the court had exceded its jurisdiction, and a man had been thus deprived of liberty without due process of law. *Richard Bourne's case* (1620) demonstrated that no local or special jurisdiction would be exempted from the control of the

---

31. Apsley's Case (1616), 1 Rolle 218, 31 E. R. 444.
32. Allen's Case (1616), Moore (K. B.) Rep. 840, 72 E. R. 940.
33. Russwell's Case (1616), 1 Rolle 218, 81 E. R. 445.
34. 10 Coke Rep. 68b, 77 E. R. 1027.

central courts.[35] Bourne had been imprisoned by the Warden of the Cinque Ports and had successfully petitioned King's Bench for a writ of habeas corpus charging that the Warden had no authority to commit him. The Warden refused to obey the writ and produce Bourne, whereupon an *alias* habeas corpus with a penalty attached for non-compliance was issued. To this the Warden answered that the writ did not run to the Cinque Ports. His stand occasioned a meeting of all the judges to discuss the point. Their combined opinion was that all the king's writs ran to the Cinque Ports and most ". . .especially this Writ which is a Prerogative-Writ, which concerns the King's Justice to be administered to his Subjects; for the King ought to have an [accounting] why any of his Subjects is imprisoned; and no Answer can satisfie it, but to return the cause. . ."[36]

A steady stream of writs of habeas corpus continued to flow from the central courts at Westminster to the London courts, justices of the peace, and other minor jurisdictions to give effect to the power of supervision.[37] In most cases the purpose of the writ's issuance was simply to supervise and restrict. However, in some cases it appeared that the judges had a very low opinion of the competency of the special jurisdiction in the first place, and they devised a very interesting technique to frustrate action. The College of Physicians of London, for example, had already encountered the power of Common Pleas in circumstances which did not produce a very favorable impression on the judges as to the judicial impartiality of the College.[38] The second time that the College and the common law met, a technique of permanent frustration was introduced.

One Dr. Alphonso had been committed by the College for the practice of medicine in London without license from the College.[39] The King's Bench issued a habeas corpus at his petition. Upon receiving the return the Bench held it to be insufficient as to cause of commitment and refused to allow time for amendment. This latter move was itself unusual, but what followed was even stranger. The judges reasoned out loud that if they completely discharged Dr. Alphonso from the College's commitment, the College would most likely re-commit Alphonso and use that as an opportunity to submit a more perfect return to a second habeas corpus. Therefor, the judges thought it best for Alphonso that

---

35. Croke, Jacobi 543, 79 E. R. 465.
36. *Loc. cit.*
37. For example, in Ellis and Johnson's Case (1632), Croke, Car. 261, 79 E. R. 828, it was held that all prceeding in an inferior court *after* the receipt of a habeas corpus were in error and coram non judice. See also Spencer's Case (1616), 1 Rolle 317, 81 E. R. 512; Rex v. Maddox (1616), in: John Tremaine, *Pleas of the Crown* (London 1723), p. 353; Hodges v. Humkin, Mayor of Laskerret (1614), 2 Bulstrode 139, 80 E. R. 1015; Webb's Habeas Corpus Case (1616), 3 Bulstrode 214, 81 E. R. 180. See: Coke, *Institutes*, Pt. IV (London 1797), Ch. VII.
38. T. F. T. Plucket, "Bonham's Case and Judical Review," 40 *Harvard Law Rev.* (Nov. 1926) 35.
39. Dr Alphonso's Case (1615), 2 Bulstrode 259, 80 E. R. 1105.

he not be absolutely discharged as requested, but rather bailed, since by bailing the court would retain a nominal jurisdiction over him, and he would be immune from the College's process. A neater solution could not be imagined.

* * * * * *
* * * *
* *
*

I think that these many instances of the use of habeas corpus against the ecclesiastical, conciliar, and minor jurisdictions demonstrate the original contention that although no new uses were evident, there was a greatly intensified use of the process. Indeed, habeas corpus was well on its way to becoming notorious as a way of escaping commitments. Significantly, habeas corpus featured in a comedy of 1608 called *Law Tricks, or Who Would Have Thought It?* Having gotten involved in a truly hilarious legal tangle, the principals speculate as to what they should do:

> Angelo: Urge a reprieve!
> Lurdo: Our punishment defer.
> Du: No we must be an upright Iustice;
>   To the execution.
> Horatio: Doe, the world shal prove
>   My heart's as bold to die as twa's
>   to love.
> Lurdo: (moaning) Dirlady so is not mine, ide
>   give my goods for a good *habeas corpus*,
>   to remove me into another Countrie.[40]

I believe also that the cases illustrate a heightened appreciation of the connection between the due process requirements of the common law and the writ of habeas corpus. But none of the cases were of sufficient general interest or fame to make this connection obvious to all. The publicizing of this aspect in such a way that lines could be drawn and emotional commitments made was left to one of the most famous and important state trials of the Seventeenth century. And it is to this case and the problem of executive commitment that I now want to turn.

Habeas Corpus and Executive Commitments

Of all the state organs none represented the royal prerogative more proximately than did the Privy Council. Its duties and responsi-

---

40. John Day, *Law Tricks, or Who Would Have Thought It?* (London 1608), act 5.

bilities were manifold, but among the most important was the exercise of that part of the royal prerogative concerned with the direct administration of royal justice.[41] In the exercise of this authority, the Council frequently committed persons without indictment, trial or any other semblance of due process as that was understood at common law. And this great gap in the protection of the subject's legal rights had long been an unhappy subject of complaint from the common lawyers. But what to do about it? Could the king's will as manifested by his Council be subjected to the scrutiny and control of the king's courts, courts whose authority derived also from the royal prerogative? Until England made a basic constitutional distinction between the Crown and the Monarch the contradiction involved in the problem of subjecting executive commitment to common law due process could not be resolved.

Council commitments and the common law courts.—This fundamental contradiction was reflected in the unclear relationship between the Council and the courts of common law at least as that relationship can be drawn out of the cases. It had been the purpose of the *Resolution of the Judges* to specify what authority the common law courts could exercise.[42] But if my interpretation is correct that document did nothing but definitively restrict the competence of the judges in any instance when the Council wished to retain custody. Specifically, when the return to a writ of habeas corpus showed only general cause of commitment (per speciale mandatum) and no specific reason, the courts could only remand. That they did not deviate from this agreement is demonstrated by later cases.[43]

That is not to say, however, that the problem of unchecked executive commitments had been laid to rest, nor to intimate that the common lawyers were reconciled to what they considered an arbitrary power of commitment. But with one notable exception the agitation for change was centered in the House of Commons, a phase we have yet to cover. This exception was *Darnel's Case* (1627), a case which under dramatic circumstances raised the entire issue, this time for public as well as judicial trial.[44]

The real background of *Darnel's Case* lies in the incredible incompetence of Charles I, who compounded folly upon folly throughout his reign. An exasperated House of Commons retaliated at one point by rolling out its biggest guns, impeachment and a refusal to grant

---

41. Edward Raymond Turner, *The Privy Council of England in the Seventeenth and Eighteenth Centuries, 1603-1784* (Baltimore 1927), p. 181.
42. *Supra*, pp. 67-69.
43. Les Bruer's Case (1615), 1 Rolle 134, 81 E. R. 382; Sir Samuel Salkinstowes' Case (1616), 1 Rolle 219, 81 E. R. 444. In both cases the Kings Bench remanded upon receipt of the general return.
44. 3 *How St. Tr.* 1-59.

supplies. The king's chief minister, the Duke of Buckingham, was impeached for breaking ". . .those nerves and sinews of our land, the stores and treasures of the King. . ."[45] Charles answered by committing Sir John Eliot and Sir Dudley Diggs, the managers of Commons' charges before the Lords, to the Tower of London. This violation of Parliamentary privilege precipitated a bitter debate parts of which indicate the thinking then current in the House:

> A king can doe no wrong because wee thinke he will doe noe wrong, and if wrong be done it is through misinformation. We must not say, because the king had done it therefore it is no wrong, but wee must examine it. [By the Resolution of the Judges of 1592] the Judges resolved that if the Queene committed any one and the Judges send an *habeas corpus* for him, the cause of the Commitment must be showen. And the king cannot deteine any one in prison above twenty-four howers without showing the cause of his imprisonment if it be demanded [according to] Magna Carta.[46]

That this was a very inaccurate statement of the existing law is not half so important as the fact that it was stated.

The result of the matter of Buckingham's impeachment was the dissolution of Parliament and no grant of supplies. When a call for voluntary gifts aroused no enthusiasm, Charles was forced to extreme measures in order to replenish the state coffers. "Some clever person," as Tanner reconstructed it, "suggested to Charles that although the Statute of Benevolences prevented him from compelling his subjects to give him money, there was nothing to prevent his compelling them to lend it."[47] This then was the genesis of the infamous Forced Loan of 1626, the occasion for *Darnel's Case* of 1627, and the prelude to the Petition of Right of 1628.

The resistance to the Forced Loan was as universal as its enforcement was harsh. Those who could not pay were either pressed into military service or compelled to billet soldiers; those who would not pay were committed by order of the Privy Council.[48] Opposition from the judges was subdued by the peremptory dismissal of Justice Crew of King's Bench, while literally hundreds were imprisoned for an offense known neither to the common nor statute law.[49] In one stroke Charles had clearly framed the issue: the royal prerogative *versus* the right of personal liberty, and to it directed the attention of the entire nation.

Darnel and four other gentlemen were among those committed

---

45. Green, *op. cit.*, Vol. II, p. 187.
46. Nathaniel Rich, *Parliamentary Diary*, Guerney Ms., fol. 90, as quoted in: Thompson, *op. cit.*, p. 326, n. 90.
47. Tanner, *op. cit.*, p. 59.
48. *Loc. cit.*; Trevelyan, *op. cit.*, Vol. II, p. 164.
49. Tanner, *op. cit.*, app. 3, p. 270.

by the Privy Council for refusing to "loan" money. Their counsel immediately petitioned King's Bench for a writ of habeas corpus ad subjiciendum arguing that the petitioners had a right to bail. The writ issued to the Warden of the Fleet who returned that the prisoners were held *per speciale mandatum Domini Regis* thereby raising the question of whether the court would continue to regard this return sufficient at law. The specific issue was whether the judges should bail or remand a man who had been committed by the King in Council without specifying the reason for commitment either on the warrant of commitment or on the return to habeas corpus.[50]

It was emphasized at the very outset by counsel for the petitioners that the writ of habeas corpus was the ". . .only means that the subject hath in this and such-like cases. . ." to obtain judicial determination of whether or not his commitment was legal.[51] Moreover, since the purpose of habeas corpus was to show the court the cause of commitment on its return, it was imperative that the return be as specific as possible. At the very least the specification of cause should be sufficiently explicit to assure the judges that the petitioners were not being held on ". . .causes for which, by the law of the kingdom, the subject ought not to be imprisoned."[52] Further the return ought to show that the petitioner had been committed through a regular process of indictment, and not by mere suggestion made to the king or his Council. Such practices were contrary to Magna Carta and the interpretive acts of the Fourteenth century.[53]

Basically, the general return *per speciale mandatum* was insufficient in that it did not state the reason behind the general cause stated in the return. The warden held the parties by reason of a special command. But this told the court nothing about the true cause, that is, what impelled the command of commitment to be given in the first instance? And lacking this how could the court determine whether the commitment was in accordance with the law of the land, or determine whether to bail or remand?[54]

But the argument which appeared to disturb the Bench most, and indeed the most fundamental difficulty of all, was the subject's lack of legal rights and remedies when he met his king in dispute. With a slight tinge of sarcasm, Serjeant Bramston summarized the issue well:

---

50. 3 *How. St. Tr.* 1-59 *passim.*
51. *Id.* at 6 (Serjeant Bramston).
52. *Id.* at 7 (Serj. Bramston).
53. *Id.* at 6, 7, 17 (Serj. Bramston).
54. *Id.* at 6, 13 (Serj. Bramston). See also Serjeant Calthrop's argument: ". . . the return of the cause of a man's imprisonment ought to be precise and direct upon the H. Corpus, insomuch as thereby to be able to judge the cause, whether it be sufficient or not: for there may not any doubt be taken to the return, be it true or false, but the court is to accept the same as true; and if it be false, the party must take his remedy by action upon the case." *Id.* at 22.

I beseech your Lordship to observe the consequences of this cause. If the law be that upon this return this gentleman should be remanded . . . if this return be good, then his imprisonment shall not continue on for a time, but for ever; and the subjects of this kingdom may be restrained of their liberty perpetually, and by law there can be no remedy . . . and therefore this return cannot stand with the laws of the realm or that of Magna Charta . . . If your Lordship shall think this to be a sufficient cause, then it goeth to the perpetual imprisonment of the king's subjects; for in all those causes which concern the king's subjects, and are applicable to all times and causes, we are not to reflect upon the present time and government, where justice and mercy floweth, but we are to look what may betide us in the time to come hereafter.[55]

Moreover, the problem was particularly acute in a cause like the instant ". . .for it being before trial and conviction had by law, it is but an accusation, and he that is only accused ought by law to be let to bail."[56]

It was the task of supporting counsel, Serjeants Noy, Selden and Calthorp, to demonstrate that the books and precedents supported Serjeant Bramston's opening arguments on the right and writ of personal liberty. Generally it was contended that the Great Charter prohibited commitment except in accordance with the law of the land, and that the phrase *per legem terrae* had come to mean exclusively process due at the common law. As John Selden argued:

The statute of Magna Charta, cap. 29, that statute if it were fully executed as it ought to be, every man would enjoy his liberty better than he doth. . . The Law saith expressly . . . *Nullus liber homo capiatur vel imprisonatur nisi per legem terrae*. My lord, I know these words "legem terrae" do leave the question where it was. . . But I think . . . it must be intended by due course of law, to either be presentment or indictment.[57]

Imprisonment merely by special command was not included in this definition of due process and was, therefor, contrary to the law of the land. And if a commitment were contrary to due process, bail, at the very least, should be allowed.[58] Serjeant Calthrop devoted himself to an elaborate exposition of the authorities such as Plowden, Fitz-Herbert, and Dyer with a purpose of establishing parallels between acknowledged practice on other processes and what ought to obtain on the writ of

55. 3 *How. St. Tr.* 10.
56. *Id.* at 7.
57. *Id.* at 18.
58. *Id.* at 14 (Serj. Noy).

habeas corpus.[59]

The entire case for the petitioners labored under the handicap that the exact question presented had never been argued before, much less resolved. Consequently none of the authorities were strictly in point. Even the *Resolution of the Judges* suffered in this respect. It could be and was used to show that it was the judge's desire and intention that all prisoners be brought before a court for judicial disposition, and the sooner the better. But the *Resolution* dealt with the question of delivery, not bail; and, more important, it did not condemn the power of commitment or the return *per speciale mandatum*. Serjeant Bramston gave explicit recognition to the fact that the legal position of the petitioners was none too secure:

> I conceive that our case will not stand upon precedents, but upon fundamental laws and statutes of this realm, and though the precedents look the one way or the other, they are to be brought back unto the laws by which the kingdom is governed.[60]

The weakness of their position was further emphasized by the fact that the precedents adduced were not precedents in the modern sense of that term. Bramston's cases were merely persuasive evidence of past practice, and not more or less authoritative and binding guides as is the case with modern precedents under the doctrine of *stare decisis*.[61]

Under these circumstances Attorney-General Heath was not hard put to demolish the petitioners' case. He demonstrated to the satisfaction of the Bench that the precedents ". . .which they have cited [were] no precedents for them."[62] And in this connection Heath made a comment which is a very good indication of the notoriety attending the trial:

> And, by Lord, it is a dangerous thing for men in matters of weight to avouch precedents with confidence, when they make nothing of them: for my Lord, precedents are now become almost proclamations, for they already run up and down the town. . .[63]

Moreover, he intimated that if the Court should hold the general return insufficient it would mean little, if any, improvement in the subject's position. For, after all, the judges could not question the truth of the

---

59. 3 *How St. Tr.* 21. For example, citing Dryer on the rule that trial pleading must be by precise affirmation, Calthrop contended that " . . . if in pleading there must be direct affirmation of the matter alleged, then a *fortiori* in a return [to habeas corpus] which must be more precise than in pleading. . . [This] return, which ought to be certain, and punctual, and affirmative, and not by way of information out of another man's mouth, may not be good, as appeareth by the several books of our law."
60. *Id.* at 10.
61. The effective doctrine of stare decisis did not develop until after this period. See: Carleton Kemp Allen, *Law in the Making* (Oxford 1946, 4th. ed.), pp. 175-224, esp. at pp. 192-200.
62. 3 *How. St. Tr.* 46.
63. *Loc. cit.*

return no matter what it was. Presumably if the general return were held insufficient the Council would merely return some non-bailable offense such as treason in order to retain custody.

But the Attorney-General's most telling points were delivered to the basic constitutional issues raised by petitioners' counsel. "I do acknowledge," Heath argued, "that the liberty of the subject is just, and that it is the inheritance of the subject, but yet it is their inheritance *secumdum legum terrae.*[64] The paramount law of the land was the absolute power of the sovereign. This meant not that the king may ". . .do what he pleaseth, for he hath rules to govern himself by, as well as your lordships, who are subordinate judges under him, "but,

> The difference is, the king is the head of the same fountain of justice, which your lordships administer to all his subjects; all justice is derived from him, and what he doth, he doth not as a private person, but as the head of the commonwealth, as *justiciarius regni,* yea, the very essence of justice under God is in him; and shall not we generally . . . submit to his commands . . .
>
> [Moreover] who shall call in question the actions or the justice of the king, who is not to give any account of them? As in this our case, that he commits a subject and shews no cause for it. . .[65]

The Attorney-General's conclusion that potential abuse of discretionary power had nothing whatever to do with its legitimacy was correct, of course, but hardly reassuring.

For the first time King's Bench found itself in the somewhat unhappy position of having to choose between two carefully defined positions. The first would have expanded the authority of the court at the expense of the royal prerogatives for the possible benefit of the subject. The second would have the court leave current and accepted practice unchanged—a course which could or could not detrimentally affect the subject's liberty depending upon the character and policies of the monarch. King's Bench took the easier and safer course. In stating the judgment of the court after a review of the major cases, Chief Justice Hyde commented:

> . . . by all of which you may see, that when the king releaseth his commandment, they were bailed for the rest, and as they were committed by the king's commandment, so they were released by the king's command.[66]

The Chief Justice did not deny that the petitioners could be bailed by

---

64. 3 *How St. Tr.* 36.
65. *Id.* at 37.
66. *Id.* at 58.

the King's Bench, but only that the court could not bail them until particular cause for the commitment were certified to the court. Until that time the judges would hold the matter under advisement, and the petitioners were remanded to custody. In short, the court had never bailed a prisoner of the king without specific warrant in the form of a specific return to habeas corpus. And King's Bench could not see its way clear to start with *Darnel's Case*.[67] The real importance of the case, then, lay in the fact that it defined issues and stirred passions, passions of sufficient strength to give men the courage to tackle head-on the fundamental constitutional problem.

The right of personal liberty and the writ of habeas corpus in Parliament.—We have in the preceding sections considered the court phase of the effort to secure universal application of common law due process standards through the use of habeas corpus. The realization of this goal floundered on the formidable rock of the royal prerogative, and the courts could go no further. Only Parliament could serve as an effective locus of opposition in such important matters, for into this one body was funneled all the discontents of all the factions of the realm. Because the various factions were thus institutionally united, the power which each could exert was supplemented by the others, and though there were differences between them, they were as one in their common opposition to the imperial pretensions of the king.[68]

Increasingly from the ascension of James I, Chapter 29 of the Great Charter was cited in the debates stirred by royal policies. The Charter was cited on behalf of the ministers deprived of their livings and silenced by the High Commission.[69] It was brought forward every time the king sought to increase revenues by levying or adjusting impositions. The exercise of such power without Parliamentary sanction was denounced as an unjust deprivation of property, and as one writer happily put it, "Englishmen did not need Locke to tell them that the chief reason why civil government was established was to protect property . . ."[70] Especially after Edward Coke assumed his leading role in the House of Commons was the Charter invoked against all manner of malodorous practices. This was particularly true as regards monopoly grants which authorized patentees to arrest and commit those who infringed their grants. It was not unusual for such authority to have been included in a patent, but the scandalous administration of some brought the whole practice into disrepute and raised the question of how to provide

---

67. 3 *How St. Tr.* 51-59 for the award and reasoning of King's Bench.
68. Francios Pierre Guillaume Guziot, *History of Civilization in Europe* (New York 1899), Lect. 13, p. 194.
69. Tanner, *op. cit.*, pp. 31-33.
70. Gough, op. cit., p. 54; S. B. Chrimes, *English Constitutional History* (Oxford 1948), pp. 144-146.

legal checks.[71]

One of the results of the debates of 1621 was the drafting of a bill ". . . for the better secureigne of subjects from wrongful Imprisonment . . . contrary to magna charta, *cap*. 29."[72] This bill, introduced November 30, 1621, had it become law would have introduced some rather radical changes in the law of habeas corpus. First it provided that no man could be committed contrary to the Charter and provided for a penalty for non-observance in the amount of "ten times so much in damages" recoverable by the grieved party. Moreover, the party issuing the warrant of commitment was to be deprived for one year the exercise of the office "by colour whereof" the commitment was ordered. Second, the bill provided that the order of commitment must contain the cause of commitment and that the party committed was to receive a copy of the cause. This section carried a forty pound penalty for non-observance, and limited pleading in any subsequent action to the causes specified in the warrant of commitment. Finally, all this was to be enforced by the writ of habeas corpus "which no judge shall denie . . ."[73]

Despite the fact that commitments for treason or commitments by any six of the Privy Council for "reason of state" were specifically exempted, the bill was still too drastic for the Commons to pass. John Pym summarized the objections on the grounds that it went too far in interfering with the discretion of the Council as well as the judges:

> (1) The saveinge of the authoritye to the Counsell too shorte. [In 1558] one was committed by two of the Counsell, [and he] procured a Habeas Corpus. The Writt was returned pro rebus ipsum Regem tangentibus, and the Judges did not forbeare to meddle anie further. [In the Resolution of the Judges] it was resolved that committment by two of the Counsel was good in Lawe.
>
> (2) That it is Very dangerous to the Judges if uppon mistakeinge in not graunting Habeas Corpus they showld bee subject to the Censure of Parliament.[74]

Nonetheless, the bill was important as an index to current thought about personal liberty and habeas corpus. Moreover, it demonstrated that there existed a considerable continuity of ideas as to the question of protecting the right of personal liberty by way of the writ.[75]

The problem of protecting personal liberty lay relatively quiet for the next few years until the decision in King's Bench on Darnel's petition for habeas corpus.[76] The demonstrated unwillingness of the

---

71 Thompson, *op cit*, p 300
72. Wallace Notestein, Francis H. Relf, Hartley Simpson (eds.), *Common Debates*, 1621 (New Haven 1935), Vol V, p 226 (hereafter cited: Commons Debates, 1621)
73. *Loc. cit.*
74. *Ibid.*, Vol. IV, p. 382.
75. *Supra*, p. 44 (Morice's Bill).
76. *Supra*, p. 59ff.

judges to move beyond the *Resolution* coupled with the dramatic, immediate seriousness of the problem of executive commitment left only one recourse. The party of liberty, as Francois Guizot collectively named the dissident common lawyers, merchants, and Puritans, turned to the Parliament for protection against the king.[77]

The Parliamentary debates of 1628 took up again the great issues presented in *Darnel's Case* and argued them not to the point of resolution, but to the point of the Petition of Right. Completely ignoring centuries of usage, the Commons asserted that because there was no provision for it in either statute or common law, the king could not fine or imprison outside the ordinary course of common law due process.[78] Moreover, the power of arbitrary general commitment simply did not comport with the fundamental principles of the common law, as Edward Coke put it, the power to impose arbitrary imprisonment degraded the freeman to the status of a ". . .tenant at will for his liberty."[79] Furthermore, could it be maintained that the common law offered less protection to the subject's personal liberty than to his personal property? And everyone recognized that one of the glories of the common law was its protection of the sacred ". . .*meum* and *tuum,* which is the nurse of industry. . ." and the proper object of law and government.[80] The difficulty was, of course, precisely the fact that the common law did protect goods better than body.

With such logic leading them on, the House of Commons passed the following Resolution on April 1, 1628:

1. Resolved . . . That no free Man ought to be committed, or detained in Prison, or otherwise restrained, by the Command of the King or the Privy Council, or any other, unless some cause of the Commitment, Detainer, or Restraint be expressed, for which, by Law, he ought to be committed;

2. Resolved . . . That the Writ of *Habeas Corpus* may not be denied, but ought to be granted to every man that is committed, etc., though it be by the Command of the King, Privy Council, or any other, he praying the same;

3. Resolved . . . That if a free Man be committed, or detained in Prison . . . by the Command of the King, Privy Council, etc., no Cause of such Commitment, etc., being expressed, and the same be returned upon an *Habeas Corpus,* granted for the said Party,

77. Guizot, *op. cit.,* p. 194.
78. 3 *How. St. Tr.* 79, 85-89.
79. *Id.* at 78. Selden echoed this striking private law analogy: "Whoever can say I can imprison him, I will say he is my villein." *Id.* at 79.
80. *Id.* at 85 (Sir Dudley Diggs). The address of Mr. Cresswell illustrates the type of argument which was fairly common: "My next reason is drawn by an argument *a majori ad minus;* I frame it thus: If the king have no absolute power over our lands or goods, then *a fortiori* not over our persons, to imprison them without declaring the cause, for our persons are much more worth than either lands or goods. . ." *Id.* at 72.

that then he ought to be delivered or bailed.[81]

Sir Edward Coke intended that this Resolution be the foundation for an act for the prevention of arbitrary imprisonment, for the specification of the common law version of *per legem terrae,* and for the provision of a statutory right to the writ of habeas corpus.

The House of Lords was aware of the dangers inherent in the general power of commitment, but was not so worried by it as to desire the rather radical redefinition of powers implicitly contained in the Commons' Resolution. The Lords' approach was embodied in a five part proposal which called for another confirmation of Magna Carta and its progeny, a royal avowal of the fundamental nature of the subject's rights of property and liberty, and a promise to secure them in "an ample and beneficial manner."[82]

These rather innocuous provisions aroused no opposition. But the last article of the Lords' proposed Resolution aroused a storm of protest in Commons:

> . . . and in case, for the security of his majesty's royal person, the common safety of his people, or the peaceable government of this kingdom, his majesty shall find just cause for reason of state to imprison or restrain any man's person, his majesty would graciously declare, that within a convenient time he shall, and will express cause of the commitment or restraint, either general or special; and upon a cause so expressed will leave him immediately to be tried according to the common justice of the kingdom.[83]

"Reason of state" was, of course, precisely the formula which Commons wished to eradicate along with its legal counterpart, the general return. In *Darnel's Case* Attorney General Heath had argued that the king required the general power of commitment to protect the state, and the argument continued in Parliament. But what enraged the House of Commons was the fact that "The power which the Tudors had used to unravel plots, was being employed by Charles I to punish men for refusing to contribute to the Forced Loan. The King claimed to possess the power for the benefit of a conspiracy-threatened commonwealth; it was actually used by him to force men to pay taxes in an extra-Parliamentary way."[84] As Sir Edward Coke succinctly said, "Reason of State lames Magna Charta." Consequently, in the face of the Lords' reluctance and the king's displeasure, the House of Commons proceded to translate its Resolution into concrete rules.

---

81. Francis Helen Relf, *The Petition of Right* (Minneapolis 1917), app. A, pp. 61-62; 3 *How. St. Tr.* 82.
82. 3 *How. St. Tr.* 167.
83. *Id.* at 163.
84. Tanner, *op. cit.,* p. 272.

However, the process of drafting a bill dissolved the heretofore solid unity of the House of Commons. It became clear that, although all agreed on the abuse, a complete concurrence on remedy did not exist. Essentially, the House divided into two groups which have been called the "opportunists" and the "reformers."[85] The opportunists argued for a bill which would require specific cause to be shown on the writ's return, but not on the warrant of commitment. And judges were to be guided in their determination of the suffiicency of cause returned by an act declaratory of the common law. This relatively mild position was taken by the opportunists simply because they did not feel that anything stronger had a chance of receiving the royal assent. The reformers, on the other hand, stuck closely to the original Resolution of April 1st, and demanded an act declaratory of the common law which would at once bind the judges in determining sufficiency of cause and evoke an admission from the king that commitment without cause shown plainly on the warrant was *in principle* contrary to the law of the land. And like the opportunists, they wished specific returns on the habeas corpus.

The fundamental difference between the two groups lay in the fact that the opportunists were primarily concerned with the problem of delivery from unwarranted commitment, while the reformers thought that the paramount concern was the prevention of arbitrary imprisonment. In truth both groups were faced with an emerging governmental system which had no place for the kind of right they wished to secure. Even the mildest proposal contained implicitly a differing conception of the commonwealth than the pure monarchy then in progress. The king had always possessed two kinds of power, ordinary and absolute. The ordinary ". . .power was to execute civil justice according to established laws; . . . The absolute power, 'most properly named policy and government,' was not restrained by laws. In all matters of state the king might act outside the law for the general good."[86] The effect of Stuart policy and such judicial positions as those expressed in the *Resolution of the Judges* and *Darnel's Case* was to maintain the absolute over the ordinary power. In short, whether the realm was to be governed according to the ordinary rules of civil and criminal justice or according to the whims of a monarch was left to a king who professed belief in divine right.

In view of all this it seems almost ludicrous that the Parliament hoped to gain the royal assent to a measure which, no matter how much it protested to the contrary, would limit the prerogative. However, the

---

85. Relf, *op. cit.*, ch. 4, pp. 24-35. Miss Relf has covered this aspect very thoroughly. What follows is a brief summary based on her work.
86. Francis D. Wormuth, *The Origins of Modern Constitutionalism* (New York 1949), p. 39.

humor was lost on Charles. Why could not the Commons put trust in the king's word, asked Charles, for:

> Ye acknowledge his trust and confidence in your proceedings, but his majesty sees not how you require him by your confidence of his words and actions; for what need of explanation, if ye doubted not the performance of the true meaning? For explanation will hazard an incroachment on . . . prerogative. What need a new law to confirm an old, if you repose confidence in the declaration of his majesty made . . . to both houses?[87]

The king was referring to his promise to uphold all the ancient laws, but he made it clear that he would go no further.

The House of Commons found all manner of gracious ways to say that they had no faith in the king's word. But an impasse had been reached. Soon there would be only two escapes from such a predicament. "One would have been the acceptance of a definite written constitution, which would leave no room for dispute about the boundary between the rights of the subject and the powers of the government . . . The other, which ultimately came about, was to accept the principle of sovereignty, but to place it in the hands of a responsible and representative parliament."[88]

But for the moment there was still a third way, compromise with the power of the throne. This compromise took the form of the Petition of Right, a proceeding which considerably weakened the claim which Parliament could press. A petition of right was normally a privately sponsored request for redress of specific grievances, and it could not be used to circumvent the ordinary manner of enacting general laws.[89] In other words, the proposals of neither the opportunists nor reformers could be effected in this manner. The only advantage of the petition procedure, aside from its chance of receiving the royal assent, lay in the fact that such a petition asking for judicial remedy was sent directly to the courts for implementation. Moreover, some of the leading members of Commons felt that the Petition would be vested with greater effect and authority in the light of Parliamentary proposals which preceded it:

> . . .the Resolutions of this house, and all our arguments and reasons against imprisonment without cause expressed . . . [would] be a great means to stay any judge hereafter from declaring any judgment contrary, especially if there by likelihood of a parliament. . .[90]

---

87. 3 *How. St. Tr.* 187.
88. Gough, *op. cit.*, p. 74.
89. Relf, *op. cit.*, p. 36.
90. 3 *How. St. Tr.* 179.

Finally into this "branch of Magna Charta," as Coke called the Petition, was carved the king's commandment: *Soit droit fait come il est desire par le Petition.*

As compared with the original Resolution of April 1st and the subsequent proposals, the Petition of Right was indeed a weak document. After reciting the usual liberty claims founded upon venerable statute and usage, the Petition asserted and supplicated:

> V. Nevertheless, against the tenor of the said statutes, and other good laws and statutes of your realm . . . divers of your subjects have of late been imprisoned without any cause showed, and when for their deliverance they were brought before your Justices, by your Majesty's writs of Habeas Corpus there to undergo and receive as the Court should order, and their keepers commanded to certify the causes of their detainer; no cause was certified but that they were detained by your Majesty's special command, signified by the Lords of your Privy Council, and yet were returned back to several prisons without being charged with anything to which they might make answer according to the law.
>
> XI. All of which they most humbly pray of your Most Excellent Majesty, as their rights and liberties according to the laws and statutes of this realm: and that your Majesty would also vouchsafe to declare, that the awards, doings, and proceedings to the prejudice of your people, in any of the premises, shall not be drawn hereafter into consequence or example.[91]

In a sense the Parliament had labored mightily only to bring forth a mouse. The immediate effect of the Petition was morally to reverse the judges in *Darnel's Case.* The right to imprison without showing cause, as well as the general return to habeas corpus, were declared to be contrary to the law of the land. But as subsequent events demonstrated, this in no way curtailed the king's power of arbitrary commitment.[92]

Practices and Problems of Habeas Corpus as Revealed in the Parliamentary Debates

But in other ways the Petition and the debates preceding it were of utmost significance. For the first time a full and public discussion of practice on habeas corpus ad subjiciendum and executive commitments took place, and all sorts of information came out which had heretofore existed only in the memories and experience of the practicing law men.

---

91. George Burton Adams and H. Morse Stevens (eds.), *Select Documents of English Constitutional History* (New York 1914), pp. 339-342.
92. *Infra*, p. 74.

First, insofar as commitment by king and/or Council was concerned, it became clear in the course of debate that practice on habeas corpus had not been highly formalized. More often than not the official court records did not show that any information as to explicit or particular cause of commitment had been received by the judges, let alone that such information was required of the king or Council. To have been formally recorded, such information would have had to appear on the warrant of commitment and/or the return to the habeas corpus. Nonetheless, it was evident that the judges were usually informed on the specific cause provoking the commitment. Being informed in an informal manner, the judges issuing the habeas corpus would award bail or deliver when justified.[93] Indeed, Judge Whitlock complained that the Commons had gone too far in its criticism of practice on executive commitments because the members did "-. . .not know what letters and commands we received, for these remain in our court, and were not viewed by them."[94]

The clarification of this informal procedure seemed to bolster the contentions of the crown in that it demonstrated that the courts did not bail or deliver without having particular cause shown. However, John Selden contrived to make a case by refusing to recognize the relevancy of the unofficial court records, and he did make a point which undoubtedly appealed to the technicality-oriented law man of the Seventeenth century:

> When no cause is set, yet bailment is alleged; then they answer divers were so bailed, but the causes appears by Paper-Books; but I never saw these Books to be Records, and Judges of Record make their Judgment in Records, and the cause only appears by Record.[95]

He was similarly close-reasoned in his contention that just because there had usually been warrant for bailing either in terms of specific return or explicit permission, this did not prove that by law prisoners of the Council could not otherwise be bailed. Even Selden, however, could not get around the fact that when the judges adopted a similar position, as in *Search's* and *Howell's Cases*, they met the Council in opposition.[96]

What all this boiled down to was the fact that none of the precedents or practices were *in stricto jure* for the common lawyers. But in a sense none were against them either. For the cases, like the

---

93. 3 *How. St. Tr.* 173 (Benjamin Rudyard).
94. *Id.* at 162.
95. *Id.* at 80.
96. *Id.* at 97-102.

Resolution of the Judges, expressed a spirit of the common law which favored the liberty of the subject in the form of a speedy trial, delivery, or bail. Intent and actual results, as far as habeas corpus was concerned, had been kept from conflicting by the informal communication of particular cause in all but important political cases. However, Charles and the Council ruptured these channels of communication between the government and the Bench by directly refusing to specify cause. And even though it was notoriously well known that men were in jail because they refused to loan the king money, the judges could not take official cognizance of it.

Many practical problems in rendering the writ of habeas corpus effective were also brought out in the course of debate. Mr. Mason's speech in Commons was not composed of speculative worries, but concrete difficulties which habeas corpus had encountered:

> The party may be imprisoned a long time before he shall be delivered . . . The place of his imprisonment may be in the furthest part of this kingdom; the judges always make the return of the Habeas Corpus answerable to the distance of the prison from Westminster; the jailer may neglect the return of the first process, and then the party must procure an *Alias,* and the jailer may be then in some other employment for the King, and excuse the not returning the body upon that process; and this may make the imprisonment for a year. And in the end no cause being returned remedy for it, nor be able to question for any injustice. . .[97]
> the party may be discharged; but in the meantime he shall have imprisonment, he shall never know the cause, he shall have no

In addition, the practice of transferring a prisoner constantly from one prison to another so that the writ never caught up with him was cited as a difficulty requiring correction.[98] Finally, the practice of re-arresting a party freed on habeas corpus whereby another writ was required, *ad infinitum,* concluded Mr. Mason's very revealing remarks.[99]

And in one final sense the Petition of Right stands as a document of extreme importance. I maintained at the beginning of this chapter that the key to understanding the Seventeenth century lay in an appreciation of a vastly accelerated pace of development. In twenty-five years more than a century and a half of slow, plodding development was suddenly and dramatically summed up. All of the difficult problems of state implicit in the use of habeas corpus ever since it was turned against other than "base" or inferior tribunals suddenly became overwhelmingly explicit. The specific definition of the connection between

97. 3 *How. St. Tr.* 184.
98. *Loc. cit.*
99. *Loc. cit.*

the right of personal liberty and the writ of habeas corpus, once tenuous, became the pressing legal problem of the day, while the difficulties of the writ were canvassed as never before.

The Petition of Right is important in this study because it culminates this long and arduous development of defining the ultimate purpose of habeas corpus. The Petition cemented in constitutional theory that no man ought to be deprived of his liberty without due course of law as administered by the ordinary tribunals of the land, and held up the writ of habeas corpus as the legal instrument by which this great purpose was to be effected. This is why, despite the many problems still to be resolved, the Petition of Right marked the end of the normative development of the writ of habeas corpus.

Part 2: The Legal Perfection of Habeas Corpus as the Writ of Liberty

Introduction

The normative position attained by the writ of habeas corpus at the time of the Petition of Right still required specific implementation. Those who favored the liberty of the subject knew what they wanted to accomplish with the writ, but they were far from possessing a completely well defined and effective tool. For political reasons, the judges gave the Petition of Right a highly restrictive interpretation which meant virtually no improvement in the actual position of the subject committed by executive command. Not until the troubled period which produced the Star Chamber Act (1641) did the judges appear to start implementing the spirit of the Petition, and even then the power of executive commitment was not substantially curtailed. It required, finally, a major attempt at statutory definition to refine and perfect the process in such a way as to realize the ambitions of earlier protagonists of the common law and the right of personal liberty.

This period covering the final years of King Charles' reign, the Interregnum, and the Restoration has been an object of examination by every constitutional historian writing on Seventeenth century England. Even the habeas corpus aspects of the period have received some attention.[100] However, for the sake of completeness and continuity, I want briefly to accentuate the high-lights of the period, to give an account of the legal definition of habeas corpus prior to major statutory definition, and finally to conclude with a short analysis of the Habeas Corpus Act itself.

---

100. Holdsworth, *History*, Vol. IX, pp. 115-125.

The Aftermath of the Petition of Right

To subsequent generations the Petition of Right has stood as one of the great documents of the English and American constitutional heritage. But to its contemporaries it must have seemed a bitter and pathetic reminder of their ineffectiveness in the face of determined monarchical power. The very first meeting of the House of Commons in the second Parliamentary session of 1628-1629 was concerned with violations of the intent of the Petition.[101] Attorney-General Heath's veiled prediction of what would probably happen if King's Bench ruled against the legality of the general commitment and return in *Darnel's Case* was proven quite accurate.[102] The Petition did, as *Darnel's Case* did not, render statement of general cause alone as insufficient in law, but this did not affect the king's arbitrary power one whit.

In place of stating general cause *per speciale mandatum* in the warrant of commitment and the return to habeas corpus, the Council substituted such charges as "notable contempts" or "insolent behavior at the Council-table."[103] In other words, the general commitment and return were gone, but not the arbitrary power of commitment. The situation was not helped at all by the servility of the judges during this period. In adopting an extremely narrow interpretation of the Petition, the judges in effect temporarily vitiated the long and arduous efforts to secure the right of personal liberty through habeas corpus. Justice Crooke expressed this restrictive view very clearly in the *Ship Money Case* (1637):

> Lastly, the concluding law is . . . the Petition of Right . . . and it was referred to my lords the judges whether this law doth give more than formerly from the king. And we were all of opinion that this law did give no more than what was formerly, and was only but a reviving of the ancient privileges of the subject; it added no more, but only revived what was formerly granted.[104]

In effect, this meant that the judges would continue to accept the statement of cause as given by the Council as *prima facie* sufficient, and the subject remained in the same position as he found himself in *Darnel's Case*, that is, without legally enforceable rights against executive commitment.

---

101. Wallace Notestein and Francis Helen Relf (eds.), *A True Relation of Every Days Proceedings in Parliament since the Beginning thereof being the 20th of January, 1628, Commons Debates for 1629* (Minneapolis 1921), p. 4 (hereafter cited: Commons Debates, 1629).
102. *Supra*, p. 62f.
103. Proceedings Against William Stroud, Walter Long, John Selden, and others, on an Habeas Corpus, in Banco Regis (1629), 3 *How. St. Tr.* 235-294.
104. Proceedings in the Case of Ship-Money, between the King and John Hampden, in the Exchequer (1637), 3 *How. St. Tr.* 826-1316, at p. 1134.

The Act for the Abolition of the Star Chamber

In the period just preceding the passage of the Star Chamber Act of 1641, a very slight flurry of judicial activity indicated that the judges were perhaps getting impatient of the transparent circumventing of the Petition by the Council. In 1639 the King's Bench bailed prisoners of Council on the ground that a mere statement of contempt was insufficient; they wanted a specification of the contemptuous words so as to judge for themselves.[105] And in 1640 the Bench bailed a man committed by the Council of the Marches of Wales. Had the judges bailed on a jurisdictional basis, it would not have been particularly surprising. But the specific reason given was their contention that the return was insufficient, which usually meant too general. In this case, however, the return to habeas corpus was exceedingly specific and detailed and the order of commitment was authorized not only by the regional Council, but the Privy Council as well.[106] Finally in *Wilnough's Case* (1640) King's Bench directly interfered with the effectuation of explicit Council orders to the Mayor of London by bailing men commited by the Mayor in pursuance of a Council directive.[107]

Whether or not these cases indicated a reassertion of judicial authority, one fact was very clear. The Parliament was again ready to impose restraints on the power of executive commitment. The crushing despotism of the years following the Petition convinced the new Parliament meeting in 1640 that a statutory attack on the problem would have to be made. Hostility focussed on the extensively employed Star Chamber and the judicial functions assumed by the Council along with its regional subdivisions. Consequently, the bill which finally emerged abolished the Star Chamber altogether, eliminated the courts held by the regional Councils, and deprived the Privy Council of all jurisdiction in civil causes.[108]

The provisions of the Star Chamber Act were to be enforced by the writ of habeas corpus. The Act provided that any man committed by the named agencies contrary to the Act was to have a habeas corpus immediately upon demand out of King's Bench or Common Pleas, that the jailer must return the writ with a statement of true cause, and that the court must take final action on the writ within three days of its return.[109] Finally, the Act adopted ideas made current long before for making the writ immediately effective.[110] *Section* 8 provided that

---

105. Barkham's Case (1639), Croke, Car., 507, 79 E. R. 1037; Lawson's Case (1639), Croke, Car., 507, 79 E. R. 1038.
106. Seele's Case (1640), Croke, Car., 558, 79 E. R. 1080.
107. Wilnough's Case (1640), Croke, Car., 397, 79 E. R. 937.
108. 16 Charles 1, c. 10, *Statutes of the Realm* (1819) 110-112.
109. *Ibid.*, sec. 8.
110. *Cf.*, Morice's Bill, *supra*, p. 44, and the proposal of 1621, *supra*, p. 65.

any jailer who failed to return the writ or any judge who failed to issue it upon a proper petition would be liable to the party "aggreived" for treble damages. As far as I know this was the first time in English legal history that a common law judge was made financially liable for the damage which an exercise of his authority might entail.

In effect then, the writ of habeas corpus was made a statutory remedy demandable as of right in all cases covered by the Act. As far as habeas corpus itself was concerned, this changed status constituted the major net gain of the Act. Unfortunately the Act did not deal with other serious problems involved in practice upon the writ, nor apparently did it seriously disturb the power of the Council to commit and retain persons in close custody. A brief five months after the passage of the Star Chamber Act, Commons was again complaining of arbitrary imprisonments and violations of the Petition of Right.[111]

The Interregnum

The years following the Star Chamber Act, the years of confusion, civil war, and the Interregnum government, are relatively scanty in their references to the writ of habeas corpus. Greater issues were the topic of discussion. An occasional case indicates that the writ operated in normal fashion in ordinary cases.[112] Certainly there is no notice of a general suspension or that petitioners were encountering other than the standard difficulties.[113]

Many of the worst features of Seventeenth century English law and administration attracted the reforming zeal of the Commonwealth parties. The corruption and venality of Chancery very nearly resulted in its abolition.[114] In the same spirit it was proposed that the "mystery," dearly beloved by the common lawyers, be stripped from the law. Richard Overton advocated in one of the Leveller manifestoes that ". . .all the Lawes of the Land (lockt up from common capacities in the Latine or French tongues). . . be translated into English tongue," and that technical phrases, abbreviations, and so on, be eliminated in order that the "meanest English Commoner" could understand his own legal proceedings.[115]

One of the major concerns of the Commonwealth was the problem of debtor relief, a problem made doubly acute by the cumulative effect of war's disruptions and high taxes. The policy of imprisoning the

---

111. *The Grand Remonstrance* (Dec. 1641), articles 11-15, in: Samuel Rawson Gardiner (ed.), *The Constitutional Documents of the Puritan Revolution*, 1625-1660 (Oxford 1906), pp. 209-210.
112. Anon. (1642), March N. R. 106, 82 E. R. 432; Heaman's Habeas Corpus (1643), March N. R. 203, 82 E. R. 476; Anon. (1649), Style 129, 82 E. R. 585.
113. *Supra*, p. 72, and *infra*, p. 80ff.
114. Tanner, *op. cit.*, p. 172.
115. Don M. Wolfe (ed.), Leveller Manifestoes of the Puritan Revolution (New York 1944), "Certaine Articles for the good of the Common Wealth," pp. 189-195, at p. 192.

debtor until such time as it appeared that his creditors could be satisfied was deservedly criticized, particularly by the Levellers, as both harsh and stupid.[116] And one result of the agitation in this regard was the lifting of the ancient ban on bailing or discharging in habeas corpus proceedings when the cause of the petitioner's incarceration was shown to be debt.[117]

In December of 1649 the Parliament enacted that any imprisoned debtor might apply for a habeas corpus to bring his case before a justice.[118] If, during the hearings on the return, the debtor took an oath of poverty,[119] he became entitled to a writ of *scire facias* commanding the presence of his creditors in order that they might show cause why the debtor should not be released. If the court released the petitioner, all his goods and holdings, excepting five pounds worth of tools, clothing, and bedding, went to the satisfaction of his creditors, and the debt was discharged. In effect, habeas corpus proceedings were made to serve as a voluntary action in bankruptcy.

Not entirely unconnected with the problem of debtor relief was the government's desire to enforce the price control laws and prevent profiteering in those commodities which were controlled principally for the benefit of the poorer classes. Civil war naturally caused dislocations in the distribution of necessities, and these natural dislocations were exacerbated by the activities of unscrupulous tradesmen and farmers.[120] The provision of London with adequate supplies of coal and grain at reasonable prices was, perhaps, the most acute problem during the period of 1648-1652. One means adopted by the Commonwealth government to cope with the situation was a series of acts (1649-1650) aimed at engrossing, forestalling, and black marketing of supplies, acts the enforcement of which was made more positive by the denial of habeas corpus and/or certiorari to those charged with their violation.[121]

Even though one can easily appreciate the justification behind this restriction of habeas corpus, it is nonetheless clear that the Commonwealth, like the Monarchy before it, had discovered that habeas corpus could be an impediment to the effectuation of state policy. And whenever a case with political implications is encountered it becomes manifest that the Commonwealth could be as oblivious to pressing legal standards

116. William Haller and Godfrey Davies (eds.), *The Leveller Tracts*, 1647-1653 (Columbia 1944), "The Case of the Armie," pp. 64-87, at p. 81; "The Humble Petition," pp. 148-155, at p. 152; "An Agreement of the Free People of England," pp. 318-328, at p. 325.
117. *Supra*, p. 23.
118. C. H. Firth and R. S. Sait (eds.), *Acts and Ordinances of the Interregnum*, 1642-1660 (London 1911), Vol. II, pp. 321-323.
119. *Id.* at 240. The oath of poverty had been defined by an earlier Act of 1649 which provided that any debtor who swore that he possessed no more than five pounds worth of real and/or personal property was entitled to release from jail.
120. Margaret James, *Social Problems and Policy during the Puritan Revolution*, 1640-1660 (London 1930), ch. 6, esp. at pp. 256-271.
121. Firth and Sait, *op. cit.*, Vol. II, p. 443.

as was the Monarchy.

Episodes in John Lilburne's running battle with Cromwell and the Commonwealth Parliaments provide ample illustrations of this contention. After the Putney Debates of 1647, Lilburne and the Levellers went into full opposition to the Commonwealth Parliament, and Lilburne's considerable talents as an agitator and pamphleteer were bent to the task of publicly discrediting that body in the hope that a strongly adverse public sentiment would topple it.[122] He was rewarded for his efforts in January 1648 by being committed to the Tower by command of Commons on a charge of having published treasonous and seditious material.

The close imprisonment of the leading Leveller merely intensified the attack on the Commonwealth government. All the old precedents once levelled against royal executive power were now fired at the Houses of Parliament: They could not, as the King could not, indict by personal command, but could initiate legal action only by writ original at the common law;[123] similarly they could not require answer or give judgment, such matters being the province of the ordinary courts of the land.[124] Moreover, whatever the charge or by whomsoever made, the prisoner was entitled to a writ of habeas corpus to test the commitment.[125] Finally, a general warrant of commitment whether authorized by King or Parliament was not good in law, and the petitioner had a legal right to bail or discharge.[126]

Despite the fact that the law of habeas corpus was clearly in his favor, Lilburne was forced to petition three times, over a period of several months, before he was allowed to come to trial in October, 1649.[127] And then he was arraigned before an extraordinary session of Oyer and Terminer rather than Kings Bench.[128] The elaborate arguments on jurisdiction, venue, and so on, raised during the trial are not pertinent here. Suffice it to say that by a shrewd combination of legal argument, histrionics, and demagoguery, Lilburne won a verdict of acquital from a jury given a directed verdict of guilty by the Commissioners of Oyer and Terminer.

However, there is one interesting aspect of *Lilburne's Case*, an aspect also present in his second court battle with the Commonwealth

---

122. Joseph Frank, *The Levellers, A History of Three Seventeenth Century Social Democrats, John Lilburne, Richard Overton, William Walwyn* (Harvard 1955), pp. 135-153.
123. University of Michigan, *English Historical Tracts*, Vol. XXXI (March-May 1648): J. Howldin, "The Lawes Subversion, or Sir John Maynards Case Truly Stated," (hereafter cited: Eng. Hist. Tracts).
124. Ibid., Vol. XXXI. "The Lawes Subversion . . ."; "The Humble Petition . . of Thomas Adams . . . Presented to the Lords at their Bar on Tuesday, April 25, 1648."
125. *Ibid.*, Vol. XXXI. John Lilburne, "The Prisoners mournfull cry, against the Judges of the Kings Bench"; Wolfe, *op. cit.*, p. 80, "A New Engagement, or Manifesto."
126. *Eng. Hist. Tracts*, Vol. XXXI, "The Prisoners mournful cry. . ."
127. loc. cit. Lilburne petitioned for a habeas corpus on April 19th, 25th, and May 1st.
128. 4*How. St. Tr.* 1270.

in 1653,[129] which has relevance to the developing constitutional ideas surrounding habeas corpus process. Unlike the men of the 1620's, Lilburne and the Levellers were not appealing to the courts and to Parliament against arbitrary executive power; they appealed to the public and the courts against an arbitrary legislative power. In the various Leveller pamphlets there is both an express and implied appeal for judicial review of legislative acts, a plea that the courts intervene between the subject and his legislature for the protection of the Englishman's fundamental liberties.[130]

In an interesting pamphlet published after the state trials of John Lilburne and John Streater in 1653, it was bluntly asserted that "Commands, because they come from Parliament are not therefore to be obeyed, but rather for the Law, Reason, and Justice in such Commands."[131] And though the writer admitted that the Upper (King's) Bench was an inferior court to the High Court of Parliament, yet "The inferior are not bound to obey the superior, but as the superior commandeth Law or Reason."[132] Specifically addressing himself to the role of habeas corpus proceedings, the anonymous author stated that:

> If an *Habeas Corpus* be of sufficient force to bring the body of a Parliaments prisoner to the Bar, that the Judges may enquire the cause of imprisonment; then if there appear no cause, the Judges cannot give Judgement for his remanding, although he be prisoner by Order of Parliament, because the Law requireth his discharge.[133]

But such contentions had no more effect on the courts of 1650 than on those of 1620.[134] The superior power, indeed dominant power, of the government, in cases where it wished to exert itself, still determined the outcome of habeas corpus proceedings.

Legal Definition and Problems of Habeas Corpus Prior to the Habeas Corpus Act of 1679

Before turning to the last stage of the writ's development, the

---

129. 5 *How. St. Tr.* 407. Lilburne was exiled by an Act of Banishment passed in 1651 for scandalous libel against a member of Parliament. He returned to England without leave and was arrested for violating the Act of 1651. He won the second trial also, using the same techniques as had proved successful in 1649.
130. *Eng. Hist. Tracts,* Vol. XXXVIII (Aug. 1650-Dec. 1653\, John Lilburne, "Lieu. Col. John Lilburne's Plea in Law, against an Act of Parliament of the 30 of January 1651." In this summary of his plea, Lilburne asserted that the Act of Banishment against him was an act, ". . . against the common right, common equity, and common reason, and therefore is void and null in law, and ought not be executed. . ."
131. *Ibid.,* Vol. XXXVIII, "Clavis ad aperiendum Carcieris Ostia, or the High Point of the Writ of Habeas Corpus discussed," unnumbered page 5.
132. *Id.* at unnum. p. 7.
133. *Id.* at unnum. p. 7 *et seq.*
134. Captain Streater's Case (1653), 5 *How. St. Tr.* 366. Streater applied for and received two separate writs of habeas corpus. He was remanded upon the return of the first due to the court's unwillingness to oppose an order of Parliament. Subsequently, on the second writ's return, he was discharged. But the discharge was due to the intervening dissolution of Parliament and the consequent vacating of its orders, not to a change of judical heart.

Habeas Corpus Act of 1679, I want to summarize the writ's legal definition as well as some of the non-political or technical problems to which the writ was subject. First, for all non-criminal matters the habeas corpus remained a judicial writ grantable at the discretion of the court. However, judging from the frequency of its appearance, it was seldom refused unless the judges felt that issuance would lead to an abuse of process.[135] Second, in commitments stemming from a criminal charge the habeas corpus had become a writ of right. This resulted from the collective impact of the Petition of Right and the Star Chamber Act.[136] The frequent employment of habeas corpus in both of these capacities was indicated by the fact that the law books began to contain numerous standard returns to the writ.[137]

The courts which could issue the habeas corpus as a test for the validity of commitment were Chancery, King's Bench, Common Pleas and Exchequer.[138] A petitioner could have the writ from Chancery or King's Bench for any cause, criminal or non-criminal, *ex merito justiciae*.[139] Exchequer could issue only for a non-criminal commitment and only if the petitioner could claim privilege.[140] The authority of Common Pleas was less clear.

In spite of the fact that Common Pleas had issued habeas corpus in cases concerning criminal commitments even prior to the Seventeenth century,[141] and was explicitly given authority coeval with that of King's Bench in the Star Chamber Act, its power to issue the criminal form ad subjiciendum was questioned after the Restoration. The doubt and confusion probably arose due to the fact that the courts made practically no distinction as to the form they used, that is, ad subjiciendum for criminal commitments and ad faceiendum for non-criminal detentions. Their practice in this regard is a perfect illustration of Maitland's observation that lawyers seldom recognize a change until it has become an accomplished fact, and that ". . .their technical terminology will but slowly admit the fact that a single form of action has become several forms of action."[142] Moreover, the period during which a distinction

---

135. This remained the case when the petition showed a commitment for debt since the enlightened legislation of 1649 was abrogated at the Restoration. An interesting *Memorandum* (1637) in Hutton 129, 123 E. R. 1150 indicates what the judges would consider an abuse of process. A petition of prisoners incarcerated in London begged for temporary release on habeas corpus so as to permit the prisoners to leave London, then being attacked by plague. The petition was referred to all the judges for comment. They condemned it, pointed out that if the prisoners feared for their safety, they could obtain release by merely paying their debts.
136. Jenk's Case (1676), 6 *How. St. Tr.* 1208.
137. John Kitchin, *Jurisdictions: Or the Lawful Authority of Courts Leet, Courts Baron, etc.* (London 1656), pp. 515-517; William Hughes, *Commentaries upon Original Writs* (London 1655), pp. 96, 108, 124; Michael Dalton, *The Office and Authority of Sheriffs* (London 1682), pp. 250-254.
138. Coke, *Institutes*, Pt. II (London 1671, 4th. ed.), pp. 52-53.
139. *Institutes*, Pt. IV (London 1671, 5th ed.), p. 290.
140. *Loc. cit.*
141. Hinde's Case (1577), *supra*, p. 31.
142. Frederic W. Maitland, *Equity, also the Forms of Action at Common Law* (Cambridge 1913), p. 347.

started to be drawn coincided with the time when notoriety attached to habeas corpus as used by King's Bench in cases of criminal commitment. The Bench used the ad subjiciendum form and it was natural that, as this form became strongly associated with criminal commitments, it would come to be considered as the special concern of King's Bench as the court principally concerned with criminal matters. At any rate by the 1670's the confusion was such that even the judges of Common Pleas were uncertain as to their authority to issue the writ in criminal matters.[143] There was no question, however, concerning the authority of Common Pleas to issue habeas corpus to test the validity of non-criminal commitments; it had been clearly doing so for several hundred years.

As Professor Holdsworth has pointed out, there was also considerable confusion regarding the question of when the various courts could issue the criminal and non-criminal forms of habeas corpus.[144] According to Coke, King's Bench, Common Pleas, and Exchequer could issue only during term of court, rendering the writ unavailable during vacation; but Chancery, being "never adjourned" could issue habeas corpus anytime.[145] But Mathew Hale provided a different set of rules.[146] And again even the judges were not positive in these matters of precise procedure.[147]

The prevailing uncertainty regarding the authority of courts could mean considerable delay and frustration for the petitioner. But this problem was by no means the most serious difficulty involved in practice upon the writ. First, even though the writ usually commanded an "immediate return," there was no way to compel the recipient to return promptly upon the first issue. If the return was not made within a reasonable time an *alias* (a second) writ was issued. But even this could be ignored, causing the service of a *pluries* writ (a third) . Meanwhile the party imprisoned received no judicial hearing. This was a complaint brought out as far back as the Petition of Right debates.[148] Another grievance voiced in the debates, and still unremedied, was the ability of jailers to transfer prisoners and thereby divest themselves of custody. If they did not have custody they could not implement the writ. This practice was common enough to warrant its own standard return to the writ.[149] A third problem was the practice of recommitting parties discharged on habeas corpus and thereby seriously curtailing any good which the writ could do. The only means which the courts had to

---

143. Jones' Case (1677), 1 Modern 235, 86 E. R. 852.
144. Holdsworth, *History*, Vol. IX, p. 116.
145. Coke, *Institutes*, Pt. II and Pt. IV, pp. 53 and 81 respectively.
146. *The History of the Pleas of the Crown* (London 1800), Vol. II, pp. 145-146.
147. Jenk's Case (1676), 6 *How. St. Tr.* 1296. The question of whether or not Chancery could issue the habeas corpus in vacation was decided in the negative.
148. *Supra*, p. 72.
149 Kitchin, *p. cit.*, p. 516.

prevent this was to bail instead of discharge.[150] Fourth, the continued unwillingness of the judges to examine the truth of the return left the liberty of the subject hanging on the veracity of the gaoler. With some luck, much persistence, and considerable funds to support legal assistance, a committed party might have been able to overcome these difficulties. However, the final device used to frustrate the operation of habeas corpus was absolutely fatal. This was the Council's practice of removing prisoners altogether out of the jurisdiction of the royal courts, removing them to "remote islands and garrisons."[151]

The Habeas Corpus Act of 1679: "An Act for better securing the liberty of the Subject and for Prevention of Imprisonments beyond the Seas."

From 1668 the Parliament had been trying to provide statutory solutions to some of the pressing problems involved in habeas corpus process, but for one reason or another no final action was ever taken on the various proposals.[152] Finally in 1679 the two houses of Parliament managed to agree on a combination of clauses designed to correct the worst of the writ's problems. This poorly drafted, confused tangle of provisions became the famous Habeas Corpus Act of 1679.[153]

I might note at the very outset that, unfortunately, the problems which were uppermost in the minds of the drafters revolved around procedure on criminal commitments in general and Council commitments in particular. Consequently the Act dealt only with criminal commitment. But the result of the Act, as Holdsworth has indicated, was to make the habeas corpus ad subjiciendum ". . .the only form of the writ used for the purpose of protecting liberty."[154] This is a bit confusing. Does it mean that the writ of habeas corpus was no longer to be used in commitments arising out of non-criminal matters?

The answer lies in the fact that after 1679 a habeas corpus used to test the validity of any commitment, criminal or non-criminal, was called habeas corpus ad subjiciendum. The cumbersome full style of the writ after this period—habeas corpus ad faciendum, subjiciendum, et recipiendum—indicates the union of previously separate qualifying phraseology.[155] However, the union of the two forms, ad faciendum and ad subjiciendum, was one of title only. There continued to be a dis-

---

150. Dr. Alphonso's Case (1615), *supra*, p. 56ff.
151. This was one of the principal charges against the Earl of Clarendon in his impeachment proceedings. See: Proceedings against the Earl of Clarendon (1688), 6 *How. St. Tr.* 291-512, at 330.
152. Holdsworth, *History*, Vol. IX, p. 117.
153. 8 *Statutes at Large* (1763) 432-439.
154. Holdsworth, *History*, Vol. IX, p. 118.
155. William Blackstone, *Commentaries on the Laws of England* (Boston 1799), Vol. III, p. 131.

tinction made between habeas corpus issued on criminal matters or on non-criminal matters. And since the Act of 1679 dealt exclusively with criminal commitment it did not legally affect practice on habeas corpus as used for non-criminal commitments.[156] Consequently, the habeas corpus used for non-criminal matters remained a common law remedy, and the solution of its problems was left to the judges and to later legislation.[157]

Understanding, then, that the Act of 1679 dealt only with problems of habeas corpus ad subjiciendum as issued to test the validity of criminal commitments, the provisions of the law can be set out.[158] And since the law lacks any organization of its own, I want to arrange the important provisions in terms of the problems attacked.

The problem of vacation and authority: All difficulties on the score of which courts had authority to issue habeas corpus at what time was settled by *Section 10*. This gave to Chancery, King's Bench, Common Pleas, and Exchequer authority to issue the writ in term time or in vacation. Moreover, if the judges of these courts, or any of them, should refuse to issue the writ during vacation upon a proper petition, the judge or judges would be liable to the petitioner in the amount of five hundred pounds.

The problem of delayed court action: Under the terms of *Section 3*, the judge or court receiving the return upon habeas corpus was given a maximum of two days to act finally upon it. Within this period the court had either to discharge the prisoner or take sureties for his subsequent appearance before the court having on its docket an action against him. Unfortunately no maximum was established on the amount of surety which the judge could demand, and the abuse of this provision was made the subject of complaint in the Bill of Rights ten years later.

The problem of delayed returns: The time-consuming *alias et pluries* procedure was destroyed by *Section 2* where time limits were based upon the distance between the issuing court and the recipient of the writ. If the recipient was within 20 miles of the court, the prisoner and the true cause had to be produced within three days. If the distance was between 20 and 100 miles, return time was set at ten days; for distances greater than 100 miles the time was twenty days. *Section 5* enforced these limits by providing that should the recipient refuse to produce the body and cause, or fail to do so within the limits set, he

---

156. Crowley's Case (1818), 2 Swanston 3-92, 36 E. R. 514-519.
157. Most notably an enactment of 1816: "An Act for more effectually securing the Liberty of the Subject," 56 *Statutes at Large* (1816) 505-508. This Act made the common law, non-criminal habeas corpus ad subjiciendum as effective as the statutory, criminal habeas corpus. It provided that the writ could issue in vacation, established sanctions to compel immediate return, and gave the judges power to inquire into the truth of the return.
158. Documentation to section is as follows: 8 *Statutes at Large* (1763) 432-439; sec. 1, p. 432; sec. 2, p. 433; sec. 3, p. 433-34; sec. 4-5, p. 435; sec. 6, p. 435-36; sec. 7-8, p. 436; sec. 9, p. 436-37; Sec. 10-11, p. 437; sec. 12, p. 437-38; sec. 13-16, p. 438; sec. 17, p. 438-39; sec. 18-21, p. 439.

would be liable to the petitioner in the sum of one hundred pounds in an action for damages. A second offense of the same nature involved a liability of two hundred pounds and removal from office.[159] The same penalty applied if the jailer refused to give the committed party a copy of the warrant showing the cause of commitment within six hours of demand.

The problem of transferring prisoners: As noted previously, two of the major complaints were directed to the practice of jailers or Council avoiding the writ by moving the prisoners. *Section* 9 cured the first ill by absolutely prohibiting the transfer of prisoners unless it was by order of some court expressed by the habeas corpus itself or some other appropriate writ. Anyone authorizing or executing an illegal warrant of removal was made subject to the same penalties attaching to refusing or delaying the return. The Council's method of avoidance was similarly declared illegal in *Section* 12, and was enforced by a provision for treble damages (not to be less than five hundred pounds) applying against anyone authorizing or executing a warrant for transferral "beyond the seas." In addition, anyone knowingly in violation of this provision would be "disabled from thenceforth bearing any office of trust or profit" anywhere in the king's dominions and would not be allowed the king's pardon.

The problem of recommitment: Section 6 provided that no person could be recommitted, once released on habeas corpus, for the same cause or any "pretended variations" thereof. In case of an absolute discharge this meant for the facts stated in the return the matter was *res judicata*. In case of bail, only a final judgment delivered by a court of competent jurisdiction over the cause stated in the return could commit the petitioner. Again a five hundred pound penalty attached for knowingly violating this section.

These then were the major problems attacked and the solutions offered by the Habeas Corpus Act. In closing it would be appropriate to note that the Act included some important exceptions to its provisions and, moreover, failed to provide an answer to one of the writ's major problems. First, as already noted, the Act in no way applied to non-criminal commitments.[160] Second, the provisions demanding and enforcing returns of body and cause did not apply to prisoners in custody for treason or felony plainly expressed on the warrant of commitment.[161] This exclusion was designed to preclude the danger of escape in these

---

159. In addition to these penalties, the Act of 1816 made non-obedience to a writ issued either for criminal or non-criminal matters punishable as contempt of court. 56 *Stat. at Large* at 506, 507.

160. This was given explicit effect in section 8.

161. Sec. 2.

more serious crimes while the jailer was transporting the party to court. Provision was made, however, whereby it would be impossible to detain without trial any person so charged for more than two sessions of court.[162] Finally, the major problem left by the Act was the failure to allow the judges to examine the truth of the return. The only recourse which a prisoner had against a false return was an action upon the case against the jailer for false imprisonment.[163]

Unlike the Petition of Right, the Habeas Corpus Act did not definitively mark the end of a period of development. The writ still faced some technical problems, such as that of excessive bail, which could temper its effectiveness. Nonetheless, the Act of 1679 did crystalize a long history of ideas respecting the legal procedure surrounding personal liberty. Despite its shortcomings, it made the writ of habeas corpus the most efficacious safeguard of personal liberty ever devised.

---

162. Sec. 7.
163. The Five Knight's Case (1627), 3 *How. St. Tr.* 34. In practice the judges managed to modify this rule somewhat, but statutory correction waited until 1816 at which time the courts were given full power to examine the truth of the return. 56 *Stat. at Large* 505, at 507.

Summary and Conclusions

The essence of constitutionalism is the notion that the government of man over man should be limited both in its spheres of competence and in its techniques of operation. But why limited government? Because in the absence of Plato's philosopher-king, man's experience has been that absolute government tends to arbitrary government. And arbitrary government leads to moral and physical insecurity, produces confusion and fear which are mortal poisons to the soul. Thus the demand for a measure of personal security is the motive force behind the progress of constitutionalism.

But constitutionalism as an operating system can make no headway until and unless the demand underlying it acquires operational specificity and techniques instrumental to its realization. Only if the demand for security is formulated in terms of specific rights and concrete procedures can it become meaningful in the daily life of man. Thus the primordial urge for security proliferates elaborate codes defining both the relationships which should obtain between private individuals and between subject and ruler.

The most immediate and basic expression of this demand for security is the right of personal liberty. This right is the most immediate because it deals with the preservation of the physical person, and it is most basic because it constitutes the foundation upon which the great structure of other rights and privileges must rest. The edifice of the legal system cannot be any more secure than its foundation permits. An effective right of personal liberty, then, becomes a necessary condition to the realization of constitutionalism in the government of man; without it the security of the individual rests in the fluctuating interstices of public policy.

It is at this point that the history of habeas corpus becomes germane to the history of constitutionalism. Even in its earliest form, the writ was a legal expression of the demand for security of person, an expression of the demand that a man not be subject to a declaration of rights and duties without his being present. Specifically, the original habeas corpus, in its several forms, was a means of securing the presence of parties involved in a dispute before a court authorized to declare the legal relationship prevailing between the contestants.

In the Twelfth and Thirteenth centuries the connection of the writ of habeas corpus with the right of personal liberty was not as proximate as later ages assumed. However, the problem of maintaining personal liberty was not as difficult as later ages experienced. This was immediately reflected in the early law of arrest and the definition of procedural norms connected with personal liberty. The norms, for example, expressed in the Great Charter were rather vague and limited in scope until the changed conditions of the Fourteenth century necessitated their elaboration in terms of emerging concepts of due process.

Changing social and political conditions from the early part of the Fourteenth century created not only an environment less favorable to personal liberty, but also the legal response to the impairment of that liberty. The administration of justice was centralized in the hands of royal courts which could and did exercise a supervisory jurisdiction over the activities of base courts. In part this jurisdiction was exercised by means of the newly created habeas corpus cum causa, a writ designed to test the validity of commitments made under the color of questionable authority or procedure. The Fourteenth century, then, produced both a more explicit formulation of the procedural norms involving personal liberty and the basic form of the writ of liberty.

From the mid-Fourteenth century the habeas corpus was used as an instrument to test the validity of commitments, and the subsequent history of the writ is really concerned with the expansion of the writ's scope and effectiveness. Or to put it another way, the subsequent history of the writ is an aspect of a progressively more secure concept of personal liberty. The Fifteenth century, for example, produced an association of habeas corpus with other legal processes which resulted in a great frequency of use in numerous different instances of challengeable commitments.

But the greatest advance in the writ's progress in terms of its serving as an instrumental guarantee for the foundation of a constiutional system occurred in the Sixteenth and Seventeenth centuries. During the Tudor period several developments took place which were of immense importance to the progress of a right of personal liberty and the writ of habeas corpus. First, religious conflict publicized the procedural norms of the common law version of the Charter and formulated an explicit connection between the instrumental virtues of habeas corpus and norms of the Charter. Second, this period was one characterized by jurisdictional conflict within the royal court system, conflict which resulted in the utilization of habeas corpus in matters with considerably greater significance than the supervision of base courts. Finally, a form of habeas corpus appeared which was used in connection with commitments ordered by the Privy Council itself.

The great significance of the Sixteenth century developments lay in the fact that they paved the way for a highly intensified and accelerated development during the reign of the Stuarts. In particular the Seventeenth century tied together the developments of the Sixteenth and brought them to completion. Most important, in this process was the fact that the Charter and the writ of habeas corpus became inextricably intertwined in the constitutional controversy of the period. In the battle against royal despotism the Charter was adduced as evidence of the illegality of arbitrary executive commitments and the writ of habeas corpus was seized upon as the most likely instrument by which such commitments could be subjected to due process. The result was the clear emergence of the Charter as the touchstone of the subject's liberty and the habeas corpus as the instrumental guarantee of his right. With the Habeas Corpus Act of 1679 England was provided with the necessary condition for the construction of a constitutional system, that is, a defined right of personal liberty and a process to protect it.

The American Reception of The Writ of Liberty

There is no doubt but that some knowledge of habeas corpus process penetrated the American colonies quite early in their history. Aside from the fact that some of the early leaders possessed English legal training and books, the writ's prominence in the conflicts of the Seventeenth century would have virtually guaranteed some recognition. Yet, I can discover no reference in colonial legal records indicating that habeas corpus as a means to test the validity of commitments entered colonial thought prior to the 1620's, although other forms of the writ appeared before that time. Previous investigators are mixed in their finding on the subject of reception. George Chalmers contended that the writ was not in use in the colonies prior to the formal extensions of the English Habeas Corpus Act to Virginia in 1710.[10] On the other hand, Professor A.H. Carpenter contended that an efficacious common law writ existed by the 1670's.[11]

It is my contention that the most famous guarantee of personal liberty in English law did not appear in the colonial development until the 1680's, and even then did not become immediately effective. The decade of the 1690's was the period of actual reception into American law. This lateness was not because

---

[10] *Political Annals of the Present United Colonies, from their Settlement to the Peace of 1753,* 2 vols. (London 1780), vol. 1, p.74.

[11] "Habeas Corpus in the Colonies," *3 American Historical Review* (1902-1903), 18-27. I must note immediately that the phrase "common law writ" as used in this discussion of the American reception does not mean the same thing as it would if used in a discussion of English development after the Star Chamber or Habeas Corpus Acts. In England, the distinction between common law and statutory writs of habeas corpus was the distinction between the writ used for commitments arising out of non-criminal and criminal matters respectively. In the colonial development, on the other hand, the phrase merely means that the writ was adopted by way of judicial use without specific statutory authorization. See also: *A Treatise on the Right of Personal Liberty and on The Writ of Habeas Corpus* (Albany, N.Y.) p.109; and William S. Church, *A Treatise on the Writ of Habeas Corpus* (San Francisco 1884), Ch. I, pt.5.

the colonists were unconcerned about issues of individual security and personal liberty, but because the process was neither practicable nor necessary in earlier times. When the writ did make its appearance it was the indirect and undesired result of late Seventeenth century royal policy as regards colonial governance. And its rapid assimilation into American state and national law revealed a profound consciousness of the relation between an effectively guaranteed right of personal liberty and the construction of American constitutionalism.

II. Early Colonial Conditions and Habeas Corpus

Any inquiry into the reception of habeas corpus by the American colonies should keep in mind that the impact of environmental circumstances tended seriously to de-emphasize questions of individual rights. The colonies were lodged in a primitive world, a world in which the social interests in mere survival must have far outweighed any social interest in personal right. The severity of the early colonial criminal law should occasion no surprise. The influence of the ancient Mosaic Law in the New England colonies, for example, reflected not only the central position of the Bible in Puritan thought, but also the fact that the Hebraic rules – rules evolved in a society struggling for survival – fitted the needs of a community trying to maintain itself in a hostile wilderness.[12]

That the exigencies of survival helped dictate the type of law and organization which exalted the community over the individual was well illustrated by the fact that the Virginia Colony, which was not particularly influenced by the Genevan Calvinism of New England, felt it necessary to operate under a truly Draconian marital law until about 1620.[13] Similarly, Connecticut imposed martial law

---

[12] See: Charles J. Hilkey, *Legal Development in Colonial Massachusetts, 1630-1686*, (New York 1910), pp. 93-111; Thomas Lechford, *Plain Dealing, Or Newes from New England* (1642) as reprinted in Massachusetts Historical Society, *Collections*, Vol.III, 3rd series (Cambridge 1833), pp. 55-128, esp. at pp. 83-87.

[13] Susie M. Ames (ed.), *County Court Records of Accomack-Northampton, Virginia, 1632-1840* (Washington, D.C. 1954), pp. xvii-xix; for one version of these Virginia law see: Peter Force, *Tracts and Other Papers Relating to the*

as late as 1636 to preserve the colony from disintegration.[14] Frequently, then, we find the colonies organized and operated like garrisons, armed and set against extinction. As the colonial settlements took root and aged, this early condition lost importance. But the final and most important factors prevailed well into the latter part of the Seventeenth century, and therefore had a crucial bearing on the reception of the Writ of Liberty.

I am referring, first to the fact that the institutional and legal structure that obtained in the colonies was such that complex legal process would have been absurd. The writ of habeas corpus presumed a reasonable separation of powers in general, and an independent judiciary in particular. But in the colonies a most simple governmental system prevailed in the earlier periods. There was a complete lack of any clear or consistent division of power, and little institutional separation of functions. One and the same body or officer might indiscriminately possess policy-making, administrative, and adjudicative functions. For example, the colonial councils, under their various names, acted as legislatures, administrative agencies, as well as courts of first and/or last resort. A choice example of this complete fusion of powers is seen in the records of the Massachusetts Board of Assistants; excerpting from the record, we read: "June 1631: It is ordered, that noe man within the limits of this jurisdiction shall hire any person for a servant for lesse time than a yeare; it is ordered, that Phillip Ratliffe shall be whipped, have his eares cutt off, fyned 40 pounds, and banished out of the lymitts of this jurisdiction, for uttering mallitious and scandalous speeches against the government and the church of Salem...; October 1632; It is ordered, that noew person shall take any tobacco publiquely, under pain of punishment..."[15] As one student put it, "The idea that a separation of powers was possible or desirable had not occurred to the founders of government in the

Origin, Settlement and Progress of the Colonies of North America...to the Year 1776 (New York 1947, reprint), Vol.III, tract 2.

[14] Herbert L. Osgood, _The American Colonies in the Seventeenth Century_ (New York 1904-1907), Vol. I, p. 306.

[15] J.Hammond Trumbull, _The True-Blue Laws of Connecticut and New Haven and the False Blue-Laws_ (Hartford 1876), pp. 334-336; Hilkey, _op.cit._ pp. 9-65.

American colonies."[16] In addition to the simplicity of governmental form, the nature of colonial law and administration, combined with the meager state of legal knowledge, contributed to the slow reception of habeas corpus. By necessity and design the colonial administration of justice was kept in an equitable mold until the late Seventeenth century.[17] The necessity arose from the facts that in many cases the complex body of English law was unsuited for colonial use, that the colonies possessed no trained bar, and had very few law books. The principal books in use during the earliest colonial period that dealt with the writ of habeas corpus were Michael Dalton's *Justice of the Peace*, Edward Coke's reading on *Magna Carta*, and possibly Dalton's *Office of the Sheriff*. The Massachusetts General Court ordered the first two as early as 1647.[18] But Dalton's *Justice of the Peace* barely mentions the writ of habeas corpus, and that in terms of its use with certiorari as a writ of error.[19] And in his handbook for sheriffs, Dalton merely noted that the writ must be properly signed by a judge, and gave some standard returns.[20] Nor did Sir Edward Coke delve deeply into the details of process, as he was interested principally in purpose and authority to issue.[21] However, this early dearth did not last long as other works such as Coke's *Reports* became available.[22] Certainly by the time the colonists felt a need for habeas corpus, they had ample information on its workings.[23]

The design that kept the colonial administration of justice in a flexible mold was a matter of royal policy and the preference of the colonial magistrature. In the royal instructions to Lord Delaware

---

[16] Osgood, *op.cit.*, Vol. I, p.168. For other examples of the high degree of fusion see: Osgood, p.35 (Virginia), pp. 103, 292 (Plymouth), p. 169 (Massachusetts); Vol. II, p.277 (New York, North and South Carolina).

[17] Paul Samuel Reinsch, *English Common Law in the Early American Colonies* (Madison 1899), pp.53-55.

[18] II *Massachusetts Colonial Records* 212, as cited in: Richard B. Morris, *Studies in the History of American Law* (New York 1930), p. 44.

[19] *The Country Justice, Containing the practice of Justices of the Peace* (London 1630), p.311.

[20] *The Office and Authority of Sheriffs* (London 1623), pp. 94-181.

[21] *Institutes*, part II, pp. 52-54.

[22] Coke's *Reports* were well known by 1633. See: Thomas Goddard Wright, *Literary Culture in Early New England, 1620-1730* (New Haven 1920), p. 123.

[23] See Notes 31, 32, *infra*.

concerning the governance of Virginia under the Charter of 1609, King James I advised:

> ...in all matters of Civill Justice you shall finde it properest and usefullest for your government to proceede rather as a Chancellor than as a Judge, rather uppon naturall right and equity than uppon the niceness and letter of the lawe, which perplexeth in this tender body rather than dispatcheth all causes; so that a summary and arbitrary way of Justice descreetly mingled with those gravities and fourmes of magistracy as shall in your discrecion seeme aptest for you and that place...[24]

And as the agitation, which led to the Massachusetts Body of Liberties of 1641 demonstrated, the colonial magistrature had no desire to be perplexed with precise rules of law and administration. They were quite aware that a considerable degree of their power rested upon the lack of a defined body of law.[25]

Finally, the problem of personal liberty was never a really crucial one until the assertion of direct royal control in the latter part of the Seventeenth century. Prior to this time, the colonists, within the structure of their legal order, were not without protection from arbitrariness in the sense of illegal commitment prior to regular adjudication. The very factors that have been advanced to explain the absence of habeas corpus, explain also why it was largely unneeded. The smallness of the communities, the simplicity of governmental form, the equitable nature of law and administration all conspired to produce a quick and summary justice. It was frontier justice in every sense of the term, and prevailed well into the latter half of the Seventeenth century, especially on the local level.

Most important for our focus and examination, it was not usual to incarcerate either before or after adjudication. The colonists were in much the same position that their ancestors experienced in Twelfth and Thirteenth century England. They lived in relatively

---

[24] See: Osgood, *op.cit.*, Valhi, p.63.
[25] See: Reinsch, *op.cit.*, pp.11ff; William H. Whitmore (ed.), *The Colonial Laws of Massachusetts reprinted from the Edition of 1680, Containing also the Body of Liberties of 1641* (Boston 1889), pp. 29-68.

closed communities with little opportunity to escape constituted authority. Their possessions and property were readily available for attachment should they fail to appear for a hearing or a trial, and they were subject to banishment or outlawry for flouting magisterial authority.[26] Indeed, the colonial courts seem to have preferred almost any form of sanction before imprisonment. Compared with the number of fines, stocks, whippings, bonds for good behavior, and so on, both pre-trial and post-conviction incarcerations were insignificant. The records of Essex County Court of Massachusetts establish, for example, that over a forty-seven year span from 1636, the court imposed a prison term only 87 times, for an average of 1.8 imprisonments per year.[27] Obviously, a very liberal system of bail and suretyship softened what appears to the 21st Century as a cold and harsh system of justice.[28] The problem attacked by habeas corpus, the problem of people languishing in jail without expeditious legal resolution of their causes did not exist in any serious form.[29]

---

[26] Banishment and/or outlawry appear to have been universally used in early colonial law. It was even used in the Dutch administration of New Netherlands. See: A.J.F.van Laer (translator and editor), *Minutes of the Court of Resselaerswyck, 1648-1652* (Albany 1922), p.120.

[27] George Francis Dow (ed.), *Records and Files of the Quarterly Courts of Essex County, Massachusetts, 1636-1683*, 8 volumes (Salem 1911-1921). See also: Allyn Bailey Forbes (ed.), *Records of the Suffolk County Court, 1671-1680*, 2 volumes (Boston 1933); "Proceedings of the Provincial Court of Maryland," *Archives of Maryland*, 1637-1650, Vol.4; 1649-1657, Vol.10; 1658-1662, Vol.41; 1663-1666, Vol.49; 1666-1670, Vol.57; 1670-1675, Vol.65; 1675-1677, Vol.66. See also: *Proceedings of the General Court of Assizes held in the City of New York, October 6, 1680 to October 6, 1682,* as reprinted in: The New York Historical Society, *Collections 1912* (New York 1913).

[28] For examples see: (1) Liberty No.18 of the Massachusetts Body of Liberties, (2) the Articles entitled "Clerkes of the writs", (3) "Suretyes and goods attached" in the Laws of 1660, (4) the Massachusetts's General Court's Order entitled "Keepers liberty to take Baile," reprinted in Whitmore, *op.cit.*, pp. 37, 139, 194, and 227. In New York under the East-Hampton laws only those committed on special warrant for a capital offense were denied the right to bail -- *The Colonial Laws of New York from the Year 1664 to the Revolution* (Albany 1896), Vol.1, p.66. And see: Julius Goebel and T. Raymond Naughton, *Law Enforcement in Colonial New York, A Study in Criminal Procedure, 1664-1776* (New York 1944), chapter 7.

[29] But there do exist some plaintive wails for justice. For example see: Raphael Semmes, *Crime and Punishment in Early Maryland* (Baltimore 1938), pp. 38-40.

These remarks directed to the contention that the writ of habeas corpus appeared quite late in colonial development should not be taken to mean that the colonists were unmindful of what they considered to be their rights. The agitation that produced the Massachusetts Body of Liberties demonstrated an early consciousness of due process requirements, and the colonists never tired of asserting that their rights were coeval with those of all Englishmen. It is not surprising, therefore, to find them, very early in their progress, looking toward the Magna Carta as a standard by which the worth of their own rights and procedures should be measured. In particular, the spirit of Chapter 29 of the Charter sounded many echoes in colonial thought and law.[30] When London from the 1670's began to abandon its policy of benign neglect and assert a new, more restrictive view of the colonists' legal status *vis-à-vis* the crown, it was inevitable that the Magna Carta, as conceived by Seventeenth century English attorneys and judges, would be asserted by colonials. Habeas Corpus was not born with the Charter, but by the 17th century it was an adopted child, and after 1670 the union created in England appeared in America to plague executive power.[31]

III. The Reception of Habeas Corpus in State and National Law

Up to the period of the late 1660's the Colonies had been able to pursue a course of more or less independent development. Communications with the mother country were slow and tedious and royal control discouragingly difficult to maintain. Indeed, only sporadically had the Crown attempted to exercise real authority in the colonies, and always, it seemed, the colonies had been saved by the emergence of more pressing problems in England. Not until the Restoration of the Monarchy did the king again turn attention to the problem of securing administrative control over His Majesties Plantations. However, by this time a strong spirit of independence

---

[30] H.D. Hazeltine, "The Influence of Magna Carta on American Constitutional Development," in: Henry Elliot Malden (ed.), *Magna Carta Commemoration Essays* (London 1917), pp. 180-194.
[31] See: Robert S. Walker, *The Constitutional and Legal Development of Habeas Corpus as the Writ of Liberty* (Oklahoma State University 1960).

had developed, especially in those colonies that had been chartered with local governments largely immune from external control. This is not to say that the colonies considered themselves as political entities somehow divorced from the realm. But, on the other hand, they could not consider themselves in the same relation to the Crown as was an English town or borough.

This spirit of independence manifested itself in many ways – hostility to the king's commissioners, passive resistance to imposed revisions of the local legal order, and so on. But it was not until the governorship of Sir Edmund Andros that serious resistance began to attend royal plans to consolidate and subordinate the colonies. Andros was serious in his determination to impose royal authority in his jurisdiction, and his ambition drove him to measures that, in colonial eyes, smacked of tyrannous illegality. In particular, his attack on existing land titles and imposition of what were regarded as unjust taxes brought tempers to a boiling point. For our concern, his most notable collision with the existing arrangements in Massachusetts resulted in the *Ipswich Tax Case (1687).*[32] Governor Andros had undertaken to levy taxes upon the townships of Massachusetts with no other warrant than an order of his Council. Ipswich, after a town meeting, declined to pay the levy asserting that it was illegally assessed. In answer, Andros had the town's minister, along with other prominent citizens, arrested for "contempt and high misdemeanor." The prisoners applied for and were refused a writ of habeas corpus and, at their trial the judges informed them that they "...must not think the laws of England follow (them) to the ends of the earth or whither (they) went." When the prisoners argued Magna Carta on their behalf, the court responded that they had no privilege other than "...not to be sold as a slave."[33] This application for and refusal of the writ has been taken to indicate that the common law writ was recognized and operating in the colonies. The proceedings, resulting from Vaughan's running battle with the governor of New Hampshire in 1684, have been similarly cited.[34] But in the *Ipswich Tax Case* the writ was explicitly denied as not being available as a

---

[32] Emory Washburn, *Sketches of the Judicial History of Massachusetts from 1630 to the Revolution in 1775* (Boston 1840), pp. 105ff.
[33] Washburn, *op.cit.*, p. 106
[34] Carpenter, *op.cit.,* p.22; Washburn, *op.cit.,* p.196.

common law right, and in the second instance there is no evidence that a writ issued.[35]

What these applications do demonstrate is that knowledge of the common law writ, and its background reasoning resting upon Magna Carta, was abroad in the land, and that the colonists were agitating for a remedy now found necessary. How much knowledge they had and the source of it can be seen in a letter from William Fitzhugh, attorney, to his client Robert Beverly dated January 1683. Beverly had been jailed by the governor of Virginia for refusing to produce the legislative journals of the Virginia House without the permission of that body. He was imprisoned in several different places, and was not successful in a petition for a writ of habeas corpus. Just before his trial, Fitzhugh wrote him what was meant to be a reassuring letter. He told his client that his right as an Englishman entitled him to the writ, and that his treatment was contrary the Magna Carta, the Resolution of the Judges, and the Petition of Right – all this supported by the constitutional writings of the great Sir Edward Coke.[36] However, his legal 'right' was not supported by Virginia's judges.

The precision of Fitzhugh's arguments and citations indicate that the colonists were quickly leaving that period when detailed knowledge of English law was exceptional, and entering one, as Edmund Burke later observed, when the study of law became an American avocation. Representative of the books colonists were ordering from England (with probable editions noted): Henry Bracton, *De Legibus et Consuetudinibus Angliae* (London, J.Moore 1640); Britton, *Britton, The Second Edition* (London, Thomas Newcomb 1670); Richard Crompton, *L'Authoritie et Jurisdiction des Courts del Majestie de la Roygne* (London, J.Moore 1637); William Sheppard, *The Faithful Councillor; or the Marrow of the Law in English, 2 vols.* (London, T.Brewster 1653, 2nd ed.). Also available were Hawkin's *Pleas of the Crown,* Hale's *Pleas of the Crown, The History and Analysis of the Common Law, and The History of the Pleas of the Crown,* as well as Thomas Wood's *An*

---

[35] Nathaniel Bouton (ed.), *New Hampshire Provincial and State Papers, Provincial Records* (Concord 1867), Vol. I, pp. 542-547, 564-569.
[36] *The Virginia Magazine of History and Biography* (1894), pp. 109-113; and see: Arthur P. Scott, *Criminal Justice in Colonial Virginia* (Chicago 1930), p. 58f.

Institute of the Laws of England, 2 vols. (London 1720). This last work contained an account of the purposes and uses of Habeas Corpus, as well as a summary of the provisions of the Habeas Corpus Act of 1679. In addition, collections of notable cases such as Coke's *Reports* and Hobart's *Reports* were available.[37] With such materials at hand, the colonists could and did argue their position with the sophistication of a London barrister. As the great historian Edward Channing put it, "So far as the (English common law) protected them from the English government and from royal officials they looked upon it as their birthright; so far as it interfered with their development, it was to be disregarded."[38]

The reception of habeas corpus into the colonial legal system was aided also by a contradiction inherent in royal policy. The crown was determined to anglicize the colonies, to extirpate non-English influences in the culture as well as to define a broad role for the King's royal prerogative, a role that was being significantly narrowed in England.[39] The efforts to subdue some of the more independent colonies like Massachusetts and anglicize others, like previously Dutch New York, produced contrary results. In Massachusetts, as already noted, the colonists were told they had no right to access the common law protection of the writ, but in New York the writ was introduced by royal officials as part of their general plan to guide the colony's legal development into English channels, thereby eradicating the lingering influence of the Dutch administration. The New York Charter of Liberties of 1683 contained the provision that "...the inhabitants of New York shall be governed by and according to the Laws of England" – a clause that was understood to embrace Magna Carta and the Habeas Corpus Act of 1679.[40] The understanding of the colonists and the Privy Council were, however, quite different. In 1684, the Privy Council disallowed the New York Charter with the terse observation, "...this

---

[37] See, T.G. Wright, *Literary Culture op.cit., passim.*

[38] Edward Channing, *The History of the United States (New York1905-1925)*, Vol.I, p. 529; Hazeltine, "The Influence of Magna Carta," *op.cit.,* p.186.

[39] George A. Washburne, *Imperial Control of the Administration of Justice in the Thirteen Colonies, 1684-1776* (New York 1923); Louise Phelps Kellog, "The American Colonial Charter," in Vol.I, *Annual Report 1903, The American Historical Association* (Washington, D.C. 1904), pp.185-342.

[40] For a general treatment see: Reinsch, op.cit., pp.30-35.

privilege is not granted to any of His Majesties Plantations where the Act of Habeas Corpus and all such other Bills do not take place."[41] The same fate met the attempts by Massachusetts and Pennsylvania to put Parliament's Habeas Corpus Act into effect. The reason given by London was that unless an act contained a specific reference to the colonies, it did not apply to them.[42] The Council's restrictive statutory construction, it should be noted, was not applied to tax acts.

The real reason was, of course, political not legal. Royal policy was "...obviously to keep the plantations in a state of subjection to the prerogative at least as of the time of James I, and the specific-reference doctrine was a useful argumentative weapon."[43] The king's long-term policy was clearly set out in the following instructions circulated among the colonial governors:

> And whereas great mischiefs may arise BY passing bills of an unusual and extraordinary nature and importance in the plantations, which bills remain in force there from the time of enactment until our pleasure be signified to the CONTRARY; we do hereby will and require you not to pass or give your consent hereafter to any bill or bills in the assembly of our said provinces of unusual and extraordinary nature and importance wherein our prerogative... may be prejudiced [until either: (1) the royal pleasure has been signified, or (2) unless the bill contained a suspending clause delaying its enforcement until the royal will was known].[44]

Habeas corpus, already then and still in ours, was classified as an "extraordinary legal remedy," and clearly fell under the royal ban. In sum, I can find absolutely no evidence to indicate that the writ of habeas corpus as an instrument to test the validity of commitments

---

[41] E.B. Callaghan (ed.), *Documents Relating to the Colonial History of the State of New York* (Albany 1856), Vol.IV, p.357.

[42] Hurd, *op.cit.,* p.111; Carpenter, *op.cit.,* p.23.

[43] Joseph H. Smith, *Appeals to the Privy Council from the American Plantations* (New York 1950), p.475ff.

[44] Leonard Wood Labaree (ed.), *Royal Instructions to British Colonial Governors, 1670-1776* (New York 1935), Vol.I, p.141.

was in use colonially during the early period.[45] The decade of the 1680's was one of agitation for, rather than use of the writ. New directions of royal policy, the abandonment of 'benign neglect,' created a need not before felt in the colonies – a need for protection against an arbitrary executive power of imprisonment.

The course of the reception from the 1690's onward is clear. The writ was received into American usage at first rather stealthily, and later openly with royal sponsorship. The sequence of events in South Carolina offers a clear example. In 1692, the colonial council adopted a bill authorizing judges to give effect to the Habeas Corpus Act of 1679. But the colony's proprietors disallowed the bill on the ground that it was unnecessary, in that the law of England already applied in South Carolina. The council did not 'adopt' the English act, it authorized, so to speak, the judges to adopt it; the proprietors disallowed not as a violation of royal instructions, but as 'unnecessary.' There is a double evasion that clearly was designed to avoid any ground that could give rise to an appeal to the Privy Council, and the explicit royal disallowance that would have followed. In the meantime, the courts of South Carolina could issue the writ as a common law remedy since they had not been explicitly told that such authority was denied. By the time the colony again took up the matter of giving the writ a firm, statutory base, royal policy had changed favorably. In 1712, the colony enacted almost verbatim the English Habeas Corpus Act of 1679.[46]

---

[45] I should note here that other forms of habeas corpus were in use before the *ad subjiciendum* form was incorporated. The Provincial Court of Maryland used the *ad respondendum* form as early as 1665 in order to secure the appearance before it of a prisoner committed for debt so that he could respond on still another matter. See: *Archives of Maryland*, Vol.XLIX, p.548, pp. 16, 66, 80, 496. Similarly, the Massachusetts Superior Court issued the habeas corpus *ad prosequendum* to remove an action from the Court of Pleas of Suffolk to its court. The use of these forms (which, by the way, were not clearly distinguished in colonial documents) probably accounts for previous views on the reception of the criminal form *ad subjiciendum et respondendum* that was the subject of the Habeas Corpus Act of 1679 and the U.S. Constitution.

[46] Edward McGrady, *History of South Carolina under the Proprietary Government, 1670-1719* (New York 1897), p.247. See also: Smith, *op.cit.*, p.475, n.29. Benjamin James, *Digest of the Laws of South Carolina to 1822* (Columbia 1822), p.161.

The same caution, reflecting an explicit disallowance, was evident in New York. There are records of the writ's use in the 1690's, but they are so incomplete and so infrequent that the authors of an extensive study of law enforcement in colonial New York concluded that the records conveyed "...an impression of furtiveness which leads one to wonder whether or not an issue was deliberately avoided.[47] The same could be said of Maryland.[48] However, there is no question but that the decade of the 1690's was the period during which the writ's process and substance, if not the name, were incorporated into colonial law.

After the first years of the 18th century, all further need for circumspection disappeared with the formal English extension of the privilege to Virginia in 1710.[49] Following instructions from Queen Anne, Governor Spotswood issued a proclamation that could legitimately be called America's first habeas corpus act:

> ...Whereas We are above all things desirous that all our Subjects may enjoy their legal Rights, You are to take especial care that if any person be committed for any Criminal matters (unless for Treason or felony plainly expressed in the Warrant of Commitment) he have free liberty to petition by himself or otherwise the chief Barron or any one of the Judges of the common pleas for a writ of habeas corpus....[50]

By 1712 similar instructional extensions gave the habeas corpus solid statutory foundation in North and South Carolina.[51] From this point the habeas corpus ad subjiciendum was rapidly assimilated into colonial jurisprudence. In the 18th century America effectively recapitulated some of England's 17th century conflicts, and the role of habeas corpus in dramatic cases of arbitrary governmental action

---

[47] Goebel and Naughton, *op.cit.,* p.503.
[48] See: Burrough's Case (1694) in: Carroll T. Bond (ed.) *Proceedings of the Maryland Court of Appeals, 1695-1729* (Washington, D.C. 1933), pp. 46, 394.
[49] George Lewis Chumbley, *Colonial Justice in Virginia* (Richmond 1938), p.72.
[50] Reprinted in Carpenter, *op.cit., p.24ff.*
[51] Labaree, *op.cit.,* Vol.I, pp.343, 336.

established it firmly in American constitutional thought.[52] Any suggestion that England would attempt to curtail the process in the New World aroused immediate and bitter complaint. For example, Jefferson cited the denial of jury trial and habeas corpus to Quebec in the Government of Quebec Act of 1774 as a tyrannous wrong in the American Declaration of Independence. The colonies condemned the government of George III "For abolishing the free System of English Laws in a neighboring Province, establishing therein an Arbitrary government, and enlarging its Boundaries so as to render it at once an example and fit instrument for introducing the same absolute rule in these colonies." The colonists were echoing the opinion of Mathew Hale, a great constitutional scholar of the period, that the writ of habeas corpus ought to run to all the king's dominions.[53] The importance of the writ in colonial thought is indicated by the fact that the writ was given statutory foundation in seven of the thirteen colonies by 1800. In at least four cases, such action preceded the American Revolution, and other states followed suit rapidly after 1776.[54] The Constitution of Massachusetts of 1780 best summarized the American attitude when it provided in Article VII that the writ of habeas corpus ought to be provided "...in the

---

[52] Two famous cases were Francis Makemie's Case (1707). For an account see: Force, *op.cit.,* Vol.IV, no.4, "A Narrative of a New and Unusual American Imprisonment of Two Presbyterian Ministers, and Mr. Frances Makemie." Another infamous trial was Zenger's Case (1733). See: 17 *Howell's State Trials* 675; also Anon., *The Trial of John Peter Zenger* (London 1763); J.F. Henry, "The Zenger Habeas Corpus: A Trial Heralding the Revolution," *Lawyer and Banker (1934), 33.*

[53] Mathew Hale, *The History and Analysis of the Common Law of England* (London 1713), p. 188.

[54] Until 1784, Virginia's habeas corpus rested upon Governor Spotswood's Proclamation. In 1784 the Assembly passed its own Habeas Corpus Act. See: *Acts Passed at a General Assembly of the Commonwealth of Virginia* (Richmond 1786), Ch. XXXV, p.19. The Carolinas' privilege rested upon the Royal Instructions of 1712. Georgia adopted verbatim the English Habeas Act before the Revolution although the exact date is not given. See: Robert and George Watkins, *Digest of the Laws of the State of Georgia* (Philadelphia 1800), p.18. Following the Revolution came Virginia in 1784, and Pennsylvania in 1785 [*Laws of the Commonwealth of Pennsylvania, 1781-1790* (Philadelphia 1793)]; New York in 1787 [*Laws of the State of New York* (New York 1789), Vol.I, p.77]; New Jersey in 1795 [*Acts of the 19th General Assembly of the State of New Jersey* (Trenton 1795), p.1024].

most free, easy, cheap, expeditious, and ample manner." For a legal statement, this has to be one of the clearest of all time, and I recommend its thoughtful consideration to all the current justices of the U.S. Supreme Court.

Perhaps the single most significant index to the unique position held by habeas corpus is the fact that it was the only legal process of its time thought worthy of explicit mention in the National Constitution. Unlike the substantive freedoms later included in the Bill of Rights, the writ of habeas corpus never made the transition from the relatively prosaic status of "immemorial right" to the more exalted plane of "natural right," but it certainly stood on the very fringe of that charmed circle. Still, there was a certain parallel between the approach toward habeas corpus and the great 18th century natural rights. Both were largely taken for granted, beyond argument, the self-evident truths of legitimate government. There was no need to restate the obvious in the new national constitution – besides, as was often mentioned, the existing state documents all had their lists. Alexander Hamilton in his defense of the newly proposed constitution cited the habeas corpus clause as one of its outstanding virtues, but even he did not claim that it was a necessary part of a moral universe.[55]

The approach was quintessentially American, that is, negative. Queen Anne, in a positive action, bestowed the privilege on her loyal subjects. The proposed new constitution granted nothing. The citizens of the new republic were assumed to have rights because, as citizens, they were part and parcel of the legal fabric of the polity. The concept of "citizen" (as distinct from "loyal subject") and the concept of "inherent legal rights" were inseparable to the 18th century republican mind.[56] Consequently, the proposed

---

[55] Alexander Hamilton, James Madison, and John Jay, *The Federalist* (Washington, D.C. 1901), Vol.II. paper no.84, pp.153. In his commentary, Hamilton relied upon Blackstone's *Commentaries* which were approaching the pinnacle of their authority in America.

[56] The Georgia constitutions from 1777 through 1798 illustrate the prevailing view that personal liberty and habeas corpus were so basic that an explicit, positive constitutional guarantee was unnecessary. In the Constitution of 1777, Art.LX, sec.4, it was provided that the principles of the English Habeas Corpus Act should be understood as part of the state constitution. In the Constitution of 1789, Art.IV, sec.4, the original provision was deleted in favor of a simple statement that all persons were entitled to the writ. Finally, in the Constitution of 1798, Art.IV,

constitution recognized the pre-existence of the citizen's right to be free from arbitrary imprisonment by limiting the government's authority to suspend the operation of the writ. The only question involving habeas corpus debated in the Philadelphia Convention of 1787, and the subsequent state ratifying conventions, was whether a suspending clause was necessary, and, if so, how it should be worded as to confer maximum protection to the citizen's right without crippling the state in case of emergency. The result was Article I, section 9, clause 2: "The Privilege of the Writ of Habeas Corpus shall not be suspended, unless when in Cases of Rebellion or Invasion, the public safety may require it."[57] The clause is so brief and, to modern ears, so ambiguous, it seems almost anticlimactic; is this brief, almost insignificant, clause the end result of about 500 years of English and American constitutional and legal evolution? The true significance of our habeas corpus clause is that it is a new beginning, not an ending. These few words carry the entire history of England's development of habeas corpus into American national law. Included in that history, now an official part of American law, are the Magna Carta, the English Petition of Right, the Habeas Corpus Act, the Bill of Rights and a library of truly great legal works from Sir Edward Coke through Blackstone. For at least the next century, when Americans confronted problems with habeas corpus process and the parameters of personal liberty, they turned to English studies of law and political philosophy. Indeed in 2006, one can still cite to the great English sources as legally "authoritative" on the meaning of the Writ of Liberty when arguing before our courts, because through Art I, section 9, "their law" became "our law."

---

sec.9, all positive reference to the privilege was eliminated and replaced by a prohibition upon suspension except in case of emergency. See: Poore, *The Federal and State Constitutions,* Vol.I, pp. 383, 386, 395 for the three constitutions.

[57] James Madison, *Debates on the Adoption of the Federal Constitution of 1787,* as included in: Jonathan Elliot, *Debates in the Several State Conventions on the Adoption of the Federal Constitution* (Philadelphia, reprint of 1941), Vol.V, p.484. For comments on the suspension clause in the Massachusetts Ratifying Convention see: 2 Elliots Debates 108. Mr. Lansing in the New York Convention moved that the federal clause be amended to prohibit suspension for more than six months. See also: Max Farrand (ed.), *The Records of the Federal Convention of 1787* (New Haven 1937), Vol.II, p.438.

However, the Constitution's clause, one that has been called the most important human rights provision in the original Constitution,[58] left the writ, as a federally recognized process, in a rather anomalous position. Lacking a system of federal courts to issue the writ, it remained for all practical purposes an exclusive concern of state law. The Judiciary Act of 1789 remedied the situation by establishing the first system of national courts, and the basic pattern that prevails to the present day. The Act provided:

> That all before-mentioned courts of the United States shall have power to issue writs of scire facias, habeas corpus... And that either of the justices of the Supreme Court as well as the judges of the District Courts, shall have power to grant writs of habeas corpus for the purpose of an inquiry into the cause of commitment.[59]

There was apparently no debate in Congress as to the desirability of giving the new national judiciary authority to issue habeas corpus; the writ appeared in the debates on the Judiciary Act only as part of the broader argument as to whether a separate national system of courts was needed.[60] The only express limitation included in the habeas corpus clause of the Judiciary Act prohibited the use of the writ to test commitments other than those "...under or by color of the authority of the United States."[61] The construction of this phrase, as well as all other problems of jurisdiction and procedure, was left to the newly authorized national judiciary to determine.

It would seem, at first glance, that this is the end of the story. The great Writ of Liberty was part of colonial/state law via the very natural process of Englishmen turning to English law to resolve their

---

[58] Zechariah Chafee, *How Human Rights Got Into the Constitution* (Boston 1952), Ch.3.

[59] 1 U.S. *Statutes at Large* 81.

[60] See the remarks of Congressmen Livermore and Stone in: 1 *Annals of Congress* (Gales & Seaton 1834) at p.828, col.1, and 857, p.857, col.1, 2. Both made the points that under state laws the right of personal liberty was well protected by habeas corpus, and that the existence of a federal court system with power to issue such writs as habeas corpus would create all manner of jurisdictional problems. They were very prescient in their last point.

[61] 1 U.S. *Statutes at Large* 81.

problems in the English settlements of America, and this process was eventually accepted by England as appropriate. The absorption of English common law and statute was followed ultimately by state constitutions and legislation that provided statutory foundation. On the national side, the writ seemed safely situated with the adoption of the United States Constitution and its implementing legislation; the Writ would be part of whatever law national officials developed from the early national period. So far, so good. However, habeas corpus was now thrust into an almost totally different legal and institutional environment and it quickly became clear that it was to be an offspring of the ancestral English tradition, not merely a seamless continuation of it.

IV. Habeas Corpus in the American Constitutional Setting

Three basic changes created the new environment within which the American writ of habeas corpus had to develop. First, Americans based all their governmental institutions upon a written constitution that uniformly, both state and national, declared itself to be, and was adopted as "the supreme law of the land." Their legal model was the charter of incorporation that created colonies in the first place, as (hopefully) profit-making business enterprises. While England had supremely important legal documents, such as the Magna Carta, the Petition of Right, the Habeas Corpus Act and many others, its system could not and does not point to a single, supreme originating instrument. Rather, England's system is founded upon traditions and legal development reaching back to Anglo-Saxon times. Moreover, the English are clear that their national preference is to "muddle on through" rather than attempt definitive and final statements. But the United States of America, as a legal entity, traces itself back, not to historic beginnings or practices, but to an originating document that declares itself "Supreme." A very straightforward logic indicates that all else must be derived from this point-of-origin in a rational, orderly, and comprehensible manner. The other side of this coin is that all governmental actions – *ALL* governmental actions – become subject to challenge on the ground that they are unsupported by Constitutional scripture. Thus, for every policy and action, the essential question becomes "Is it constitutional?"

Constitutional Supremacy and Habeas Corpus: This basic question arose in the context of habeas corpus proceedings *via* the case *Ex parte* Bollman (4 Cranch 75, 1807). Specifically, the issue raised was whether, in the light of the Supreme Court's decision in Marbury v. Madison (1 Cranch 137, 1803) the Judiciary Act's authorization for the Supreme Court to issue writs of habeas corpus was constitutional. The Marbury case held that Congress could not, through the Judiciary Act of 1789, expand the *original* jurisdiction of the Supreme Court by granting it the authority to issues the writ of mandamus requested by petitioner Marbury. C.J. Marshall argued that to allow such authorization would be tantamount to permitting an ordinary statute to amend the Constitution, in this instance it's definition of the Court's *original* jurisdiction. This would place the Constitution and the statute on the same juridical plane. But the Constitution declared itself to be "supreme law of the land" (which judges took an oath to uphold) and it could be amended only through the constitutionally described amending process; Congress could enact a statute only in pursuance of its terms, and Congress had not been given the authority to expand the *original* jurisdiction of the Supreme Court. Therefore, that portion of the Judiciary Act purporting to enlarge the power of the Supreme Court statute was unconstitutional, that is, unenforceable at law. This case was the beginning of a distinctively American contribution to constitutional thinking throughout the world – the doctrine of judicial supremacy.

Perhaps the argument that denied Marbury's petition for a writ of mandamus applied also to Bollman's petition for a writ of habeas corpus. Not so, answered C.J. Marshall. He distinguished the earlier case by arguing that that it presented a case involving the constitutionally defined *original* jurisdiction of the Supreme Court, while Bollman's petition was for an application of the Court's statutorily defined *appellate* jurisdiction. Bollman was *appealing* for a *review* of the legality of his incarceration – the classic use of habeas corpus. The *appellate* jurisdiction was, by Constitutional text, subject to definition by Congressional statute, indeed, the very existence of a federal court system and its power rest squarely upon Congressional statute. The Constitution establishes only the Supreme Court and gives it only a limited original jurisdiction; all other courts in the system, their original and appellate jurisdiction, and their relationship to the Supreme Court are defined under an original grant of legislative authority to Congress. In any case, the essential question is answered, the Supreme Court (and the lower federal courts) may issue the writ of habeas corpus because Congress had authorized it. A closing thought: what can be given can be taken away![62] As a matter of national law, the edifice of protection from the Writ of Liberty rests upon the shifting sands of congressional-executive politics and the support given it by the traditions embedded in the public mind. Americans should never take their personal liberty – or the major instrument that protects it – for granted.

Federalism and Habeas Corpus: The second basic change presented by the new American environment resulted from the fact that the Framers adopted a federal territorial-governmental organization departing from the unitary mold of England and the rest of the 18th century world. There was only one government of England, France, Russia, Italy, Spain and so on. The United States, on the other hand, commenced its constitutional existence with fourteen governments, and the thirteen original states were themselves divided into frequently very independent counties and cities. Further, the states generally copied the organizational schema of the national constitution, though there was no requirement that they had to. We end, after some 200 years, with a staggering number of jurisdictions and agencies. Why did we start down this road in 1787? Actually there was no choice. The states existed prior to the adoption of the Constitution, and, indeed, were needed to ratify it. Any solution to the problem of territorial organization for governmental purposes had to recognize that fact. Thus, for some purposes the United States is regarded as one unit over which the National Government is the dominant, sometimes exclusive, governor, for other purposes governing power is shared by the nation and the state, for still others the state and local system is dominant. The system is complex and constantly changing as new problems emerge and new political/legal alignments are formed.

---

[62] The Detainee Treatment Act of 12/2005 stripped the Federal Courts of all jurisdiction to hear or consider petitions for habeas corpus filed by aliens imprisoned by the Department of Defense at Guantanamo Bay, Cuba.

Given this, it should occasion no surprise that practice on a legal process such as habeas corpus, which was available at both the state and national level after the Judiciary Act of 1789, was, and will continue to be, a source of real difficulty in defining the relationship between the state and national court systems.

The major early question was whether the state or the new national courts could issue the writ to test the validity of a commitment made under the other's process. The earliest answer was to prohibit a national habeas corpus to test state commitments,[63] but to allow state courts to test federal commitments through their process.[64] This resulted in the peculiar situation of permitting state courts to determine, in particular instances, the validity of federal processes and law,[65] while disabling the national courts from discharging a state prisoner held in violation of the National Constitution or laws.[66]

---

[63] Ex parte Dorr, 3 Howard 103 (1845). Section 14 of the Judiciary Act 1789 was construed to bar federal habeas corpus to test the commitment of a party convicted in a state court.

[64] The lack of any federal statutory impediment or Supreme Court rulings left it up to the state courts themselves to decide whether they had such authority. The prevailing view was that a state test, via habeas corpus, of a federal commitment was a valid exercise of state judicial power. See: Hurd, *op.cit.,* 165-167.

[65] See: Thomas Sergeant, *Constitutional Law* (Philadelphia 1822), p.82, "It seems to be the general opinion that from a decision by a state court or judge on Habeas Corpus, in a case arising under the Constitution, Law or treaties of the United States, no appeal or writ of error lies to the United States Supreme Court... Yet, it seems the subject is within the power of Congress, and it might provide for the appellate power of the Supreme Court in such cases."

[66] See: Elkison v. Deliesseline, 8 *Fed.Case 493, no.4,* p.356 (Charleston, South Carolina 1823). This case involved the Federal government in a very embarrassing situation *vis-à-vis* England. It arose over the fact that So.Carolina authorities arrested a Negro British seaman. In 1822, the stated had enacted that "...if any vessel shall come into any port...of this state, from any other state or foreign port, having on board any free Negroes... such free negroes... shall be seized and confined in gaol until such vessel shall... depart the state." Adding insult to injury, the state act made the vessel's captain liable for the cost of confinement and subjected him to heavy penalties if he should leave without his charge. J. Johnston, in the U.S. Circuit Court, was of the very clear opinion that the state law was unconstitutional, but he was just as sure that there was no way to alleviate the situation with a habeas corpus to state authorities.

Not until 1871 could it be said that this situation was rectified. By virtue of several acts of Congress and two Supreme Court rulings, the relationship was completely reversed. Following on the heels of South Carolina's Nullification Ordinance, Congress provided in 1833 that the federal courts could protect federal agents by issuing writs of habeas corpus in any case of confinement for an act done or omitted to be done in pursuance of federal law or judicial process.[67] Another gap was filled by the Act of 1842 that gave the national courts authority to issue writs in all cases of aliens confined for acts done under authority of their government, or under international law.[68] Finally, in 1867 as part of the Reconstruction Program, Congress granted the federal courts authority to issue habeas corpus "…in all cases where any person may be restrained of his or her liberty in violation of the Constitution, or any treaty or law of the United State."[69]

Accompanying these Congressional expansions of federal judicial authority, were Supreme Court cases restricting the states' judicial ability to interfere with federal process by way of habeas corpus. In *Ableman v. Booth* (1858) the Court denied state power to discharge federal prisoners or to, in any way, by habeas corpus interfere with the processes of federal courts or agencies.[70] Many state courts retaliated by applying a very restrictive interpretation to these cases, forcing the Supreme Court to elaborate its decision in *Tarble's Case* (1871), a case in which the court issued a comprehensive prohibition to such uses of state judicial power.[71]

The complete reversal finalized by *Tarble's Case* by no means signaled the end of difficulties in defining the inter-court, national-state relationships as regards the use of habeas corpus. In 1958, for example, the U.S. Senate considered a bill, passed by the House, designed to curtail sharply the use of federal habeas corpus

---

[67] "Act further to provide for the collection of duties on imports," 4 U.S. *Statutes at Large* 634, Ch.57, sec.7.

[68] "Act to provide further remedial justice in the Courts of the United Sates," 5 U.S. *Statutes at Large* 539, Ch.257, sec.1.

[69] "Act to amend the Judiciary Act of 1789," 14 U.S. *Statutes at Large* 385, Ch.257, sec.1.

[70] Ableman v. Booth, and US v. Booth, 21 Howard 504.

[71] 13 Wallace 397. In an 8-1 decision, CJ Chase dissented. He felt that this ruling constituted an unwarranted restriction of state judicial power. If the courts erred, he said, correction was possible by appeal.

to test state convictions claimed to be in violation of the due process requirement of the 14th Amendment. This bill was a Congressional response to the Supreme Court's decision in *Brown v. Allen* (1953) that allowed a state prisoner to institute habeas corpus proceedings in the Federal District Court to test the validity of state commitment even though the Supreme Court had previously denied his petition for a writ of certiorari to review the case.[72] The 1953 initiative on behalf of state power failed, but those interested in curtailing the power of the national courts joined forces with those who wished to promote a greater degree of decisional finality and managed to secure, in 1996, some apparently sharp limits on the power of the federal courts to issue writs of habeas corpus in cases where the state courts were those of first instance. This act, the "Antiterrorism and Effective Death Penalty Act (called AEDPA)" introduces significant restraints on national judicial power in favor of state judicial power. Some of its clauses are reminiscent of the early 18th century approach, and contests regarding the juridical meaning and impact of its clauses will be adjudicated before a Supreme Court much less sympathetic to an expansive vision of national authority than was the Warren Court that produced *Brown v. Allen.*

Separation of Power and Habeas Corpus: Finally in this summary view of the impact of America's radically different setting for habeas corpus, is the fact that we adopted the idea of "separation of powers" as the basic structural principle of government. This concept was popularized by an influential French treatise, *The Spirit of the Laws*, published by Charles de Montesquieu in 1748. I think it fair to say that every member of the Constitutional convention had either read, or was familiar with the argument of this book. Montesquieu argued that there were three essential tasks involved in governing a nation: first, decisions were required regarding whether to act and, if so, what to do (the legislative job); second, decisions had to be carried into effect on a day-to-day basis (the executive job); and third since execution would always, in the course of human affairs, lead to arguments about everything connected to the

---

[72] Brown v. Allen, 344 U.S. (1953). In effect, the proposed bill would have nullified this decision, and limited the test of the constitutionality of a state commitment to a direct appeal. See: *Hearings,* Subcommittee on the Judiciary, House of Representatives, 84th Congress, 1st Session, "Habeas Corpus," 1955.

original decision and its execution, a method of resolving arguments in a more-or-less final and authoritative way was required (the judicial job). Politicians of the time recognized that a government so organized might be inefficient, but considered that human liberty was the more important value. Liberty rather than efficiency would be promoted by giving each of these tasks to a separate branch of the government, forcing them to combine their intelligence, expertise, and energy to work in unison for the good of all, and most importantly giving each a check upon the action of the other two.

In the context of our times, Montesquieu's formulation has an almost primary-school, textbook quality. It seems quaint and altogether too simple, even simple-minded, but in the 18th century it was a revolutionary departure from the historically universal practice of legitimating those who could seize and hold power with various theories of centralized authority – the cup of history overflows with Divine Pharaohs and Alexanders, Caesars, Emperors, Dictators, and Kings, like England's William I, the Conqueror. The American republic's experiment with separation, rather than fusion of powers was a 'first,' but it was and remains a very complicated 'first.' The writ of habeas corpus, like all other governmental processes, has to run the maze it created.

A. Words & Construction: Nowhere are the problems generated by separation of powers for habeas corpus more clearly seen than in the issue of suspending access to the writ. As noted earlier, it is a bit surprising, given the importance of habeas corpus in Anglo-American political and legal thinking, that there was so little attention given it in the debates at Philadelphia, and in the text of the Constitution itself. Nor did it figure in Madison's composition of the Bill of Rights. Everyone simply assumed that it had an assured place in the legal scheme of things, and the major problem was to demand that it not be suspended without grave cause – thus Article I, section 9: "The privilege of the Writ of Habeas Corpus shall not be suspended, unless when in Cases of Rebellion or Invasion the public Safety may require it."

The Constitution is supreme, thus this is basic text, and every word plus the implications of every word, must be taken seriously. From the words themselves, several tentative conclusions can be drawn. First, that access to the writ is a privilege granted by the legal order, not a fundamental natural right, such as freedom of speech. As mentioned before, habeas corpus never made the ideological transition from an "immemorial right of Englishmen" to a "natural right of man." President Jefferson would have approved that transition; he felt that the lack of a positive habeas corpus clause in the Bill of Rights was a major oversight. On the other hand, the mere mention of the writ in the Constitution gives it a singular status that distinguishes it from other important legal processes such as writs of error, certiorari, quo warranto, and mandamus, as well as from those writs authorized by Congress in creating and defining courts inferior to the Supreme Court.

Second, the words clearly imply that access to the writ can be suspended for sufficient reason – otherwise, why limit the power? However, the clause does not indicate how the relevant decisions should be made regarding whether there is an "invasion," or "rebellion," or that the "public safety" of the nation is in jeopardy. These are not self-defining terms, particularly in the 21st century. Was 9/11 an invasion? If so, where is the combatant state that, presumably, the Jihad hijackers represented? For that matter, the Civil War was never a "war," since neither the Union nor the Confederate Congress ever declared it so.

Should, the President, as the Commander-in-Chief and the highest national officer concerned with enforcement and safety, be allowed to define the terms (and thus become the *de facto* suspending authority), should Congress incorporate in a suspending act the factual situation required to trigger an executive order, or should both President and Congress defer to the Supreme Court's definitions and conclusions made in the process of considering appeals from citizen or alien prisoners taken into custody while contending with an 'invasion,' or 'rebellion'?

Third, since the limitation on the suspending power appears in Article I, the Congressional Article, it can fairly be implied that the limitation applies to Congressional authority, even though no specific Congressional power to suspend the writ is listed in Article I, section 8. However, it should be noted that this is a reasonable, not necessary implication. President Lincoln, for example, argued that the general war power given him in Article II, was sufficient to justify a suspension by Presidential Proclamation when the public safety required it, and that Article I, section 9 did not necessarily suggest that *only* congress could suspend the writ.

Fourth, the limitation on suspension does not apply to the states; constitutional provisions applying to states are listed in Article IV and make no mention of habeas corpus. On the other hand, the Supreme Court could incorporate habeas corpus into the meaning of the 14th Amendment's Due Process clause, as it has already done to large chunks of the Bill of Rights. If it were to do this, then federal review of state suspensions or denials would be assured whether or not Congress extended the power by way of defining the federal courts' jurisdiction.

There are only 26 words in the seemingly clear and simple habeas corpus statement of Article I, but they have produced endless problems in application, even though the writ has been suspended only six times in our national history. President Lincoln, by proclamation, suspended the writ in critical military theaters in 1861 and 1862. Approximately 14,000 people were arrested by the military on charges of aiding and abetting the rebellion; they could not petition for a habeas corpus to test their commitments. His suspensions occasioned much criticism, and the constitutionality of independent Presidential action was challenged. Consequently, in 1863 he obtained an Act of Congress authorizing suspension, but that act did not convey the virtually unlimited authority that the President wanted, and was itself open to interpretation. President Grant issued a suspending order for part of South Carolina upon the authority of the Ku Klux Klan Act. The government of the Philippines did so in 1905 to deal with a domestic insurrection, and the Governor of Hawaii likewise in 1941, to confront a possible invasion after Pearl Harbor.

B. Lincoln & Civil War: From all the judicial decisions generated by these actions, only one rule seems to be firmly established – that the president has no independent authority to suspend the writ. This was the opinion of major scholars before President Lincoln's actions in 1861 and 1862,[73] and their judgment

---

[73] See: George C. Sellery, Ph.D., *Lincoln's Suspension of Habeas Corpus as Viewed by Congress* (Madison, Wisc.1907), U. of Wisconsin History Bulletin, vol.1, p.213: Justice Joseph Story, *Commentaries on the Constitution of the United States* (1833) Bk.3, sec. 1336; C.J. Marshall in *Ex parte* Bollman, 8 US 75 (1807)

became part of two decisions that now have the status of settled constitutional law, precedent virtually irreversible except by formal Amendment. The first was not a decision of the Supreme Court, but of Chief Justice Roger B. Taney sitting as the presiding judge of the Fourth Circuit Court of Appeals back in the days when Supreme Court justices actually left the District of Columbia and rode circuit. In *Ex parte* Merryman (1861), the Chief Justice issued an elaborately documented and reasoned opinion holding that the President had no independent, discretionary authority to suspend the writ, and he felt duty bound to free the petitioner (then in Union military custody) even though he well understood that he had no way to enforce his order.[74] President Lincoln responded to the Merryman decision with a shot across the bow of the entire system of civil courts. In a Proclamation of September 1862 he ordered, first, a suspension of habeas corpus throughout the nation and, second, authorized the use of military courts to try all persons "guilty of any disloyal practice giving aid and comfort to rebels." His final suspension for the entire nation was in September of 1863, but this time it rested upon Congress' Habeas Corpus Act of that year.

Out of these actions arose the second major habeas corpus – separation of powers case, *Ex parte* Milligan (1866).[75] Lambdin P. Milligan, a civilian resident of Indiana was arrested and tried by military tribunal, found guilty of giving aid and comfort to rebels, and sentenced to be hung.[76] He petitioned the Federal Circuit Court for Indiana for a writ of habeas corpus to release him from military custody as his trial, he argued, was conducted in violation of terms found in the Habeas Corpus Act of 1863. A divided Circuit Court certified the case to the Supreme Court. After detailed argument from counsel for the petitioner and the government, Justice Davis delivered the opinion of a divided Supreme Court.[77] It is a ponderous and sometimes confusing decision, but it is fair to say that the administration lost the case. The president's authority as commander-in-chief to establish military districts could not displace

---

[74] 17 Fed.Cas. 144 (1861).

[75] 71 US 2 (1866).

[76] Military tribunals are *not* courts martial. Their process is less strict and formal.

[77] The Court was unanimous on the matter of habeas corpus, but split 5-4 on the issue of military courts martial jurisdiction.

the authority of the regular courts in areas, such as Indiana, where they were open and operating. If they were open, then they could hear a petition for habeas corpus, although they might, under the right circumstances, deny a release. The court sustained the reasoning of C.J. Taney in the Merryman Case that the suspending power lay with Congress, but even Congress' authority could not suspend the privilege where civil courts, as in Indiana, remained open and union authority was established. The two cases had no impact in their time; Lincoln ignored the Merryman decision, and the Milligan case was delivered in 1866, a year after the war was over. However, they did set the law for the future. Lincoln was the first, and the last, president to claim an independent, discretionary power to suspend the writ of habeas corpus and subject civilians to military trial and/or confinement. President Grant who suspended the writ in South Carolina in 1877 did so under the clear authority of the Ku Klux Klan Act of 1871.

The loss of the 19th century presidential bid for power over habeas corpus, the confirmation of the Congressional status as pre-eminent, and securing a role for the judiciary even in a time of armed conflict seem signal achievements. However, in truth, presidents since Lincoln have not been hampered by the loss. The Congress has generally been subservient when confronted by the Commander-in-Chief, the Supreme Court has usually, as in the Milligan case, issued relevant rulings reluctantly and late.[78] Presidents, for their part, have been inventive in devising ways to circumvent habeas corpus process and act decisively in emergencies, leaving it to subordinate officials to sort out whether action was constitutional or not.

C.. Roosevelt & WW II: A clear example was President Franklin Roosevelt's Executive Order 9066 of February 1942, two months after Pearl Harbor, which authorized the Secretary of War to define military areas from which any and all persons could be excluded. Congress confirmed his order in the following month. The entire West coast was so designated by the General for that district, and all persons of Japanese ancestry were "excluded." About

---

[78] For example: The legality of the suspension of the writ and the imposition of martial law in Hawaii after Pearl Harbor was not ruled upon until it no longer mattered: Duncan v. Kahanamoku, 391 US 304 (1946).

120,000 people were forced to leave their homes and businesses for internment camps; about 70,000 were American citizens, and one-half the total were children. It is estimated their property loss, without due process of law, amounted to five billion dollars. The Executive Order established military commissions (not courts martial) to hear complaints and suspended the writ of habeas corpus for those affected. By 1943-1944 cases appealing criminal convictions under the Order did reach the Supreme Court, and, in those cases, Hirabayashi v. U.S. (1943) and Korematsu v. U.S. (1944) the Supreme Court upheld the government's actions (sustaining curfews and internment camps).[79] Not until almost 40 years later, did further investigations and proceedings reveal that the military had doctored and/or falsified much of the factual information used in its own commission hearings, and later in the government's argument before the Supreme Court. In the 1980's the convictions in both cases, through *coram nobis* proceedings, were overturned as having been based on errors of fact that, had they been known during the original proceedings, would probably have led to a different decision.[80]

These cases stand as a reminder that executive-military arrests, commitments, and quasi-judicial proceedings should always be regarded with suspicion. This is not to suggest that the executive in all of its divisions, including military, needs to be regarded as underhanded, devious, or evil in any sense. It is merely to recognize, as Montesquieu and the Framers did, that the focus of the executive is upon effective, efficient enforcement of policy and targeted goals, not upon the doing of justice in individual cases. Executive and military officers of all ranks and degrees acting as judges have a long history of failure – failure to be fair judges.

---

[79] 322 US 214 (1944).

[80] *Coram nobis* proceedings cannot be used to attack findings in law, only findings in fact. Such actions are used to correct errors resulting from incomplete or false information at the time of trial. Thus, technically, the Supreme Court's decision in 1944 remains 'good' law, even though most deplore it. See: Hirabayashi v. US, 8282 F.2nd (9th circuit, 1987); 586 F.Supp.769.

D Bush & Jihad: This lesson takes on special relevance when we move into the 21st century and consider the policies of President George W. Bush as they impact the doing of justice in general, and the uses of habeas corpus in particular. The story commences on September 11, 2001 with the suicide attack on the World Trade Center and the Pentagon by Jihad members of al-Qaida, the Islamic terrorist group led by Osama bin Laden. The audacity of the attack, its success in N.Y. and D.C., as well as the national vulnerability it revealed stunned the nation. President Bush received from Congress, only one week later, the most unlimited authorization ever given an American president in peace or war. Public Law 107-40, "Authorization for Use of Military Force," contains the famous 'blank-check:

> Section 2 (a): That the President is authorized to use all necessary and appropriate force against those nations, organizations, or persons he determines planned, authorized, or committed, or aided the terrorist attack that occurred on September 11, 2001, or harbored such organizations or persons, in order to prevent any future acts of intentional terrorism against the United States by such nations, organizations or persons.

With this encouragement, the President followed up with an "Order on the Detention, Treatment, and Trial of Non-citizens." Bush's Executive Order reached back in history to a technique of extreme control used by his predecessors, Presidents Lincoln and Franklin D. Roosevelt. He revived the use of military tribunals or commissions, directly responsible to him as Commander-in-Chief, or his designee, in order to detain, try, and punish those believed to be a danger to the state and/or its Administration and policy. President Bush authorized military commanders to establish tribunals modeled upon those formed during WW II, which, in turn, echoed those created in the Civil War. He did promise that they would not be used to try U.S. citizens. However, *sub silentio*, there turned out to be one exception – the exception being a citizen designated by him as an "enemy combatant."

The Congressional authorization of PL 170-40 does not specifically authorize these tribunals, either independently or as substitutes for regular courts-martial or the civil courts. President Bush, supported by Vice-President Cheney as well as Secretaries Rumsfeld and Ashcroft, contended that such tribunals were extensions of the President's commander-in-chief powers, and, as such, were legitimated by American history and legal precedent. However, the Constitution creates only two kinds of courts: The Supreme Court in Article III, and a system of inferior Federal civil and military courts authorized by Congress under Article I. A tribunal or commission is, in effect, a Presidential or "Article II court;" such a court, by whatever name, must be considered an exception to separation of powers, a Katrina-level breach in the constitutional levies that are supposed to contain executive power. On June 29, 2006 a Supreme Court majority ruled that the President had neither independent constitutional authority nor express statutory authority to establish military commissions (tribunals) for the trial of Guantanamo prisoners.[81]

In the Declaration of Independence, President Jefferson denounced executive trials and tribunals, and three cases – one from Lincoln, one from Franklin Roosevelt, and one from George W. Bush – illustrate why he denounced them. They also indicate how dangerous to the citizen are clashes among the three branches, as well as the role of the writ of habeas corpus in providing some review and restraint of executive action. The first two are historic: (1) the trial of Sioux-Dakota soldiers in the Dakota War of 1862, (2) the 1945 military trial of General Tomoyuki Yamashita, Japanese commander and governor of the Philippines, and finally (3) a case of our time, 2002 to the present (as of this writing unfinished), the trial of Jose Padilla, Islamic Jihadist.

The Dakota Indian Wars: The Dakota Indian troubles in Minnesota had multiple causes, some going back decades. The record is full of the usual stories of White duplicity, trader corruption, and broken promises as well as lack of control by tribal chiefs. The immediate cause of the 1862 uprising was widespread hunger due to the fact that national payments for tribal lands ceded

---

[81] Hamdan v. Rumsfeld, 546 U.S. __ (2006 – No.05-184)

to Whites, were late in arriving. Young malcontents began stealing food, settlers retaliated and as many as 800 settlers died as the violence spread. Minnesota's governor commissioned Colonel Henry Sibley to organize and lead troops to quell the uprising, which, after two months of fighting, he accomplished in late September 1862. Sibley was left with about 1200 prisoners who were believed to have participated in the war plus many times that in angry settlers who wanted to hang them all.

On his own military-executive authority, Sibley established a five-man military commission to try the prisoners. The Indians were not accorded prisoner-of-war status (even though they were Dakota-Sioux soldiers), but rather were considered "wandering brigands and guerrillas" not entitled to claim the privileges of combatants under the rules of war. The commission held hearings for about six weeks, processing 20-40 cases each day. To say the least, the procedures were perfunctory, there was little of what could be called 'evidence' or 'defense' even for a military or civilian trial of that day, no member of the court or prosecution understood the Dakota language and only a few of the Indians, on their side, could speak even a 'pidgin-English'. The result was a sentence of execution for 303 of the prisoners.

The commission forwarded the verdicts to Washington, D.C. for approval. Lincoln conferred with Henry Whipple, the Episcopal Bishop of Minnesota who had traveled to Washington expressly to speak for the Indians. The Bishop was able to give the President a fuller understanding of the uprising, trial, and sentence – the sad details from the Indian perspective. The President had clerks select out those prisoners whose trial record included murder, rape, and/or massacre of settlers, and signed an order of execution for 39, while the remainder (about 86%) had their sentence commuted. On the 26th of December thirty-eight losing Sioux-Dakota soldiers, chanting death songs, were marched by victorious Union soldiers to one large circular scaffold and hanged together.[82] In 1866, President Johnson ordered the release of surviving prisoners. Almost to the day, 28 years later, the last of the Sioux Indian wars with the United States took place at Battle of Wounded Knee, S.D. In any case, the 'trial' and execution of the Dakota soldiers holds the record as being the

---

[82] One more was commuted between Lincoln's order and execution day.

largest single execution in American history. It remains controversial to this day whether recourse should have been had to the regular state or federal courts, or to regular courts martial, but these were not options considered by Colonel Sibley at the time, and no one dared to petition for habeas corpus on any prisoner's behalf. The event remains a chilling look at a military commission or tribunal in virtually unhindered operation.[83]

The Yamashita Case: The second example concerns the trial of General Tomoyuki Yamashita by a military commission created by General Styer, U.S. commanding general in the Philippines. General Styer acted at the orders of General Douglas MacArthur, overall Army commander for the SW Pacific theatre. The commission consisted of five officers of 'general' rank, none of whom had any legal background or experience in military or civil trial, nor was any of rank equal to or higher than that of the defendant, although that is standard in military trials. General MacArthur accompanied his order with a detailed set of procedural rules and guidelines for such matters as defining 'proper evidence,' many of which were quite at variance with standard courts martial procedure. In addition, six officers with legal training were assigned as defense attorneys from a pool in the Judge Advocate General's office.[84] Yamashita surrendered on September 2, 1945; his trial commenced on October 8; the military commission issued its guilty verdict and death sentence on December 7, 1945 – the 4th anniversary of Pearl Harbor.

There were major problems with the commission's work, most of which were duly considered by the Supreme Court upon a petition for habeas corpus filed by defense counsel. In their habeas corpus petition, counsel for Yamashita raised three main problems: (1) the legality of the commission, (2) the many dubious rules of procedure and evidence from MacArthur's instructions, and (3) the fact that Yamashita had been convicted for violating no law of war

---

[83] For studies of this episode see: Carol Chomsky, "The United States-Dakota War Trials, A Study in Military Injustice," 43 Stanford Law Rev. 13 (November 1990); Douglas Linder, "The Dakota Conflict Trials" [www.law.umkc.edu].

[84] For an interesting memoir from a member of the defense team and, later, a distinguished Wyoming attorney see: George F. Guy, 4 Wyoming L.J. 153 (Spring 1950) [www.supremecourthistory.org/myweb/81journal/guy81.htm].

that existed at the time of his command, but rather an entirely new rule devised by the prosecution and accepted by the commission for the purposes of the trial.

The Supreme Court in a divided vote (6-2 [1]) denied the petition for habeas corpus on the ground that the writ was properly suspended in a war zone and, by doing so, confirmed Yamashita's conviction. The Court responded to the first two matters by noting that since a state of war technically still existed between Japan and the United States at the time of Yamashita's trial (surrender did not equal a peace treaty), a military commission and its special rules of procedures were properly authorized by the President. The fact that their rules of procedure did not comply with the Constitution's trial and evidence standards was irrelevant. As to the last charge, the most charitable thing that can be said of C.J. Stone's majority opinion is that it is very confused, and seems to miss entirely the point that what was involved in this case was a kind of criminal *ex post facto* law that is clearly forbidden by the Constitution. That is to say, General Yamashita was being tried, sentenced and executed for failing to do something, rather than doing something, and this "failure" had never before been described nor subject to punishment in the law of war, general international law, or the law of the United States.

These and other points were the focus of two exceptionally strong dissents by J. Murphy and J. Rutledge. As J. Rutledge put it, "Never before have we tried and convicted an enemy general for action during hostilities... much less have we condemned one for failing to take action. The novelty is not lessened by the trial's having taken place after hostilities ended and the enemy, including the accused, had surrendered." In effect, the dissents saw the military trial as a kangaroo court imposing a 'victor's revenge.' The Supreme Court's decision to deny the petition for habeas corpus was followed by an appeal to President Truman. The new president passed the buck to General MacArthur. MacArthur sustained the decision of his military commission and hanged his former adversary.[85]

---

[85] In re Yamashita, 277 US 1 (1946). J. Stone for the Court. JJ. Murphy and Rutledge dissented. J. Jackson did not participate.

The entire point of elaborate rules of evidence and procedure is to give the defendant a fair chance of presenting another view, one that raises reasonable doubt as to guilt. In any criminal (and most civil) actions the government has the advantage. It may spend years and millions in investigations before bringing charges. Then you, the defendant, must present a defense. If you are very wealthy, very famous, or very lucky you may meet or even cancel the government's advantage, but it is not likely. Time, expertise, and money are usually the keys. In the Yamashita case, the defendant spoke no English, surrendered under orders from his government, and had never met his defense team (which was very conscientious) until a few weeks before the trial. Most of the trial's time was dedicated, by the five generals' sitting as judges, to first-person recollections of atrocities committed by Japanese troops gone wild after a complete breakdown of communications and command within the Japanese Philippine army due to intense bombardment. The military commission managed the trial in such a way as to present a finding of guilt, and a sentence of death, on the exact anniversary of Pearl Harbor. The timing suggests that motives of vengeance might have well have vied with a duty to be just.

There was one facet of this episode that neither the military commission nor the Supreme Court examined, and that was the possibility of undue command influence on the trial commission from General MacArthur. It is a matter of record that General MacArthur maintained a lively interest in the proceedings, often urging his subordinate generals to take a broad view of proper evidence, and directing his headquarters staff to urge an "expeditious resolution" of the matter. In a trial before a regular court martial or civil court, his interest and suggestions might have produced either a contempt citation or the declaration of a mistrial. Perhaps lurking in the background of his interest was personal history that, in other circumstances, would have required the General, in the interest of justice, to recuse himself from all connection to the trial. Certainly, if the trial had been a court martial under the Uniform Code of Military Justice, or in any civilian court, he would have been required to recuse himself. He was so personally involved in the events of which Yamashita was a part, that a reasonable person could question his ability to be fair

General Douglas MacArthur was the son of General Arthur MacArthur, a distinguished officer, a WW I Medal of Honor recipient, and a Governor-General of the Philippines. Douglas' first assignment upon graduation from West Point in 1903 was to the Philippines as an engineer. From that post he toured Asia as an aide-de-camp to his father, and was, of course, treated royally. When he retired from U.S. active service in 1937, he was awarded the Philippine's highest rank, Field Marshall, and given important military functions by its government. He was a close friend of Manuel Quezon, the Philippine president, and ultimately was awarded every high distinction and medal that the Philippine government had to offer.

He was living in Manila when the U.S. Army, at President Roosevelt's order, recalled him to active service and gave him command of the Philippine military. His job was to resist an expected Japanese invasion in 1941. That invasion was launched the day after Pearl Harbor. It was well planned, well supplied, and successful. For the first time in his life, Douglas MacArthur had to flee – he was forced into an ignominious nighttime escape through Japanese controlled waters in a PT boat, ultimately to establish new headquarters in Australia. He vowed to return, and return he did in 1944. But his recapture of the Philippines proved embarrassingly slow and difficult, especially in view of the brute military power he now commanded; it took longer than planned, involved much heavier casualties than expected (60,000 US, 300,000 Japanese, 1,000,000 Filipino) and slowed the advance of American power across the Pacific. MacArthur's problem was General Yamashita, known as the Tiger of Malaya for his brilliant campaign capturing the Malay Peninsula. Japan gave Yamashita the task of fortifying the Philippines against an inevitable American attack. In doing so, he mounted what military historians consider history's outstanding example of a hold-and-delay action, a strategy that had the purpose of keeping the enemy at bay (from the Japanese home islands) for as long as possible. MacArthur never succeeded in forcing Yamashita to surrender; he surrendered the Philippines only at the orders of his government, and on the same day that an atom-bombed Japan signed its unconditional surrender aboard the USS Missouri. In a sense, MacArthur lost in both directions, leaving and returning, and cannot have regarded the Philippine part of his record happily. Perhaps

Yamashita's hanging was some consolation. And perhaps that is a very unfair suggestion. The point really is this: without a fair trial bringing out the evidence before independent judges, questions linger forever.

Jose Padilla, Islamic Jihadist, 2002-??: On May 8, 2002 Jose Padilla disembarked at Chicago's O'Hare Airport completing a trip through the Middle East, Pakistan, and Afghanistan. He was arrested by U.S. officers on a 'material witness' warrant alleging he might have information relevant to terrorist attacks within the United States. From Chicago, he was jailed in the Metropolitan Correctional Center of the Federal Department of Justice in New York City, and later appeared before Federal District Judge Michael B. Mukasey who had issued the warrant. Padilla was committed for preliminary investigation and Donna R. Newman was appointed on May 15th his defense counsel. His arrest and processing over the next four years, introduces a new dimension into our review of executive/military trial and punishment and the use of habeas corpus. That new dimension is American citizenship.

The legal mind loves categories and classifications. The organic human being is broken into parts: a person may be "parent," or a "voter," or a "citizen," or an "alien." If an "alien," then perhaps a "resident" or an "illegal" one. A person might be the "testator or beneficiary" of a will, or a "tortfeasor," or a "felon" or, indeed, fit into any of thousands of labeled boxes. Each of these boxes has defined "properties" that describe all those included therein, for example, all the people in the "U.S. voter" box will be of a minimum age, possess "citizenship," not be in the "felon" box," and so on. The wonderful thing about this approach is that it saves thinking about specific people – results flow automatically from position and membership, and seem, at first glance, to be fair and just. For example, in the case of the Dakota Indians fighting the United States, the matter was much simplified by classifying the combatants not as "soldiers" but as "marauding brigands or guerillas," – a classification that hardly entitled those within it to a hearing, much less a "trial" in the constitutional sense. Similarly, General Yamashita was put into an entirely new box, one labeled "war criminal." Defense attorneys were allowed to file a habeas corpus petition to the Supreme Court, but the Court would hear only jurisdictional questions. Did the military tribunal have jurisdiction to try a foreign military war criminal? If so, then the Court could not consider whether, in fact or law, Yamashita was guilty as charged.

The Court decided, over dissents, that the military tribunal did have jurisdiction, and the new classification foreclosed further inquiry. General Yamashita was an enemy alien and a war criminal. The Indian combatants, for their part, were members of Tribal Nations as defined in treaties, not citizens. The court looked into the boxes and found no guarantee of a fair trial as prescribed by the Constitution for either. The best box to be in bears the label "citizen" – historically if a person is found in that box then he or she is entitled to the extraordinary array of legal protections guaranteed by the Constitution and the Bill of Rights, protections defined and refined over centuries.

However, to combat terrorists both in the U.S. and abroad, the Bush administration has added still another box with the label "enemy combatant," defined by the Department of Defense as anyone "...part of or supporting Taliban or al-Qaida forces or associated forces." This new box, as we shall see, has some disturbing connections to the "citizen" box, as well as properties that seem derived from the practices of police, rather than, democratic states. One of those properties was a claim of Presidential authority *not to try at all*, but simply to hold a person, citizen or not, in indefinite military custody. As a form of executive trial and punishment, this goes beyond even the extreme action of President Roosevelt in 1942 when he personally selected all the personnel (the judges, prosecutors, defense counsel) of the special military tribunal for eight German saboteurs (including one naturalized American citizen), put ashore from a submarine. He also retained personal authority to review any appeal. The President was judge, jury, and, as it turned out, executioner.[86]

But where to place Jose Padilla? Neither a Dakota Indian nor a Japanese or German national, he was born in Brooklyn – you cannot get more American than that! He is clearly in the "citizen" box. He is also a petty, violent street criminal (felon), who, from the age of 14 has been in and out of jail. It is probable that in one of his taxpayer supported stays, he found Allah and became a Muslim

---

[86]Approved by the Supreme Court: *Ex parte Quirin, 317 US 1(1942).*

Holy Warrior dedicated to destroying infidels (who, I am sure, he held responsible for his failure in life). He turned from a life of crime to a life of terrorism – thankfully unsuccessful in each calling. His ambition was to explode a 'dirty-bomb,' to contaminate a city, destroy a building or whatever target presented itself.[87]   His ambition did attract the support and encouragement of al-Qaida as well as the attention and surveillance of several governments. Indeed, unbeknown to Padilla, he was surrounded by agents posing as fellow passengers on the flight to back to the U.S.A., where he was arrested. Had the agents simply whisked him away, kidnapped him, there would have been no case for us to review. But they did execute an arrest warrant that brought Padilla within the peripheral view of the regular court system.

The constitutional problems commence at this point, because it quickly became clear that the Bush administration did not want to indict Mr. Padilla and bring him to trial by either military tribunal or regular court (the usual paths), but did want to incarcerate and interrogate him. On May 22nd, Padilla's court appointed defense counsel Donna R. Newman, seeing that her client had not been charged with anything at all, asked Judge Mukasey to vacate the arrest warrant, and the judge set June 11th for decision. But on June 9th, government lawyers, in a private meeting, asked Judge Mukasey to vacate the original arrest warrant that they had used to arrest him. They disclosed that President Bush had, on that day, officially designated Padilla an "enemy combatant," and ordered Secretary of Defense Rumsfeld to detain him. Their position was that this classification suspended Padilla's civil rights and authorized his transfer to military custody. Mukasey complied, and Padilla was conveyed, in the middle of the night, to the Consolidated Naval Brig in Charleston, S.C. He was to remain there for the next 42 months.

The next day from Moscow, Attorney General John Ashcroft announced to the world that a major and very dangerous al-Qaida operative had been captured in the United States. According to Ashcroft, this al-Qaida trained agent, Jose Padilla (a.k.a. Abdullah al Muhajir) had planned and made preparations to explode dirty-

---

[87] The so-called "dirty-bomb" is a conventional bomb to which some radioactive materials have been attached. When the bomb explodes, the other materials scatter contamination.

bombs in several unnamed American cities. On the very next day, June 11th, the date originally set to rule upon the Padilla's request to vacate the arrest warrant, his attorney was informed that the District Court no longer had custody of her client, but that he was being held, incommunicado, in the Naval Brig at Charleston, S.C. Attorney Newman then filed a petition for a writ of habeas corpus naming President Bush, the Secretary of Defense and Commander Marr of the Naval Brig as respondents. Judge Mukasey set December 4th to rule upon the arguments for and against granting the petition.

This petition for habeas corpus on behalf of Jose Padilla launches one of the most important disputes of American constitutional history, one with ramifications and possibilities no one can accurately foresee, but one, the resolution of which, will impact the lives and liberties of every citizen.[88] In her petition, Attorney Newman challenged Padilla's arrest and commitment without hearing or trial as violations of the 4th, 5th, and 6th Amendments, and argued that the government's position with regard to the designation of someone as an "enemy combatant," amounted to an unlawful suspension of the writ of habeas corpus. Furthermore, she argued that since (1) the civil courts were open and operating, (2) martial law had not been declared, and (3) Congress had not suspended habeas corpus, then the detention of Padilla had no basis in law and he should be released.

The government did not respond in detail to the points in Newman's petition. Rather it chose to assert (1) that she had no standing to act as Padilla's agent in a petition for habeas corpus, (2) that the District Court had no jurisdiction to hear the petition, and (3) that "The legality of Padilla's military detention as an enemy combatant is confirmed by historical tradition, by the established practice of the United States in times of war, and by longstanding decisions of the Supreme Court and other courts. The rule is settled: the military has the authority to detain an enemy combatant for the duration of an armed conflict."[89]

---

[88] Judge Mukasey's 105 page Order and Opinion on the Petition: United States District Court 02 Civ. 445 (MBM), Opinion and Order s/ Judge D. Mukasey; in: http.//files.findlaw.com/news.findlaw.com/wp/docs/padillabush120402opn.pdf.
[89] Underlining mine. This passage from the government's reply is found on page 3 of J. Mukasey's statement of its position in his Order cited above.

J. Mukasey's order affirmed that Attorney Newman could lawfully represent Padilla, and should be given access to him for consultation (with proper safeguards relating to sensitive security information). Further, the judge affirmed (1) Secretary Rumsfeld as an appropriate respondent for a writ, (2) his court's jurisdiction, and (3) the President's authority to detain individuals in circumstances such as displayed in the instant case, his detention of Padilla, was not *per se* unlawful. Whether it could be sustained after appropriate judicial inquiry into the causes for the Presidential order, was left unanswered until the time that such an inquiry became necessary.

Judge Mukasey's Order and Opinion was appealed by the Department of Justice to the 2nd Circuit Court of Appeals.[90] The government was especially troubled by the assertion by the District Judge of an authority to examine the rationale of the Presidential Order in order to determine whether the designation of Padilla as an "enemy combatant" had reasonable basis. The Circuit Court upheld the District Court on all points save one. It overruled J. Mukasey's holding that the President's detention was not *per se* unlawful, and ruled that it *was* unlawful. The appellate decision was, then, a clear victory for Padilla.[91]

In 2004 the Padilla Case reached the U.S. Supreme Court for the first time. Clearly it was a case that pitted the presidency against the court system – the government's arguments constituted a major assault upon separation of powers and the writ of habeas corpus. Just as clearly the Supreme Court dodged the bullet. In a 5-4 decision involving three sets of opinions, and some arcane rulings involving jurisdiction, the Court reversed the Circuit Court's decision that the District Court had jurisdiction to hear Padilla's petition for habeas corpus, and also that Secretary Rumsfeld was a proper respondent. A petition for habeas corpus would have to be filed in the district with jurisdiction in the area of the Charleston Naval Brig, and the proper respondent would be Commander Marr as she was the person with actual custody of Padilla. Having denied the jurisdictional legality of original proceedings, the Court felt no

---

[90] Padilla v. Rumsfeld, 233 F.Supp. 2d 564 (S.D.N.Y. 2002)
[91] Padilla v. Rumsfeld, 352 F. 2d. 695 (2d Cir. 2003)

need to reach the more serious questions relating to Presidential authority and whether it was subject to judicial scrutiny.[92]

The next stage of the legal drama shifts to South Carolina where, in July 2005, Padilla's attorneys filed a second petition for habeas corpus with District Judge Henry Floyd. After hearings, he ruled that the President does not have the authority to detain a U.S. citizen without trial or charge – Padilla incarceration violated the Constitution and the laws of the U.S., and he must be criminally charged or released. His decision was appealed to the 4th Circuit Court where a three-judge panel led by Judge J. Michael Luttig delivered an opinion in September supporting Presidential power completely.[93] Overruling the District Court, J. Luttig's decision argued that the President may, on his own authority or under the blanket authorization of PL 140-70, seize U.S. citizens while engaged in civilian pursuits, within or without the territory of the United States, and hold them indefinitely in military confinement without criminal charges or trial. The ruling elevates the president's war power to a general police power, and this whether or not Congress had declared war. The president need only determine that the U.S. is involved in hostilities and the person detained participated in those hostilities. In such cases, the courts would have no jurisdiction to intervene on behalf of the individual's constitutional rights.[94]

The decision of the three-judge panel of the 4th Circuit gave the government everything it wanted; indeed, its findings were so completely favorable to President Bush that the court was accused of partisanship rather than adjudication[95]. However, as far as the government was concerned, there were problems. First, the decision was very vulnerable in reasoning, statutory construction, and the breadth of presidential power validated. Second, the government's victory made appeal to the U.S. Supreme Court a certainty, and that appeal would necessarily have to confront the stark question posed

---

[92] Rumsfeld v. Padilla, 542 U.S.426 (2004).

[93] Padilla v. Hanft – Hanft is the officer who replaced Marr as Commander of the Naval Brig.

[94] http://files.findlaw.com/news.findlaw.com/hdocs/
docs/padilla/padhnft22805opn.pdf.

[95] Judge Luttig was on Bush's short list of possible nominees to the Supreme Court. On May 10, 2006, he resigned his judicial post of 15 years.

by the decision: Did the President really have the power to arrest and imprison a U.S. citizen merely by designating him an "enemy combatant" in a memorandum to the Secretary of Defense, and hold him as long as the President certified that the nation was engaged in "hostilities"? There would be no way for the Supreme Court to dodge the bullet, as it had in the first Padilla Case, and when the issue was put as starkly as this, would the government have a good chance of winning?

The Bush administration apparently decided that the matter was politically too explosive and legally too chancy. Consequently, in November 2005 the President rescinded Padilla's "enemy combatant" status, instructed that he be returned to the custody of the Department of Justice, and be indicted and tried like any other citizen accused of breaking the law, four years after he was arrested in Chicago. There is only one way of expressing what happened next – "it hit the fan." When the government appeared before 4th Circuit seeking routine approval for Padilla's transfer, Judge Luttig, for the court, refused it, and released an opinion that excoriated the Department of Justice for its behavior in the case, warning the President that he risked losing all credibility with the public at large and with federal courts hearing terrorism cases.

The 4th Circuit Court had swallowed the government's presentation of Padilla's terror-history, together with its interpretation of the applicable law, and regurgitated it in the decision. Now, only a month later, that same government announced that it was abandoning the entire case it had presented. J. Luttig and the court felt badly used, and stated that the Department's behavior "suggested" that the government was really attempting to avoid a Supreme Court review of the Circuit Court's decision. Ordinarily lower courts do not seek review, but the 4th Circuit clearly felt that its decision was necessary, correct, and defensible on appeal. However, Attorney-General Gonzales now referred to its decision as "moot" – a terrible word choice. In law school, a "moot court" is one that argues fictitious cases; a "moot" case, at best, is one that is currently irrelevant. The Circuit judges' response was understandable on a personal level, but injudicious both in language and law; there is no precedent for a court refusing a request such as was filed, and the U.S. Supreme Court, at Attorney-General Gonzales' request, overruled it in January 2006 (its second confrontation with this case).[96] The Supreme Court did retain jurisdiction to hear argument on the merits. However, on April 3, 2006 it dropped this residual interest by failing to muster the four votes needed to accept an appeal. Echoing the Attorney-General, some of the justices declared that, since the 4th Circuit decision was now "hypothetical," there was no basis to consider appeal – they dodged the Padilla bullet again. Technically, the Court's non-action leaves the decision as "good law" for the 4th Circuit.

Consequently, Padilla is finally to be tried in September 2006 in the Miami District Court of Judge Marcia Cooke. The charges against him bear no resemblance to those announced by Attorney General Ashcroft in 2002 – there is no mention of "dirty bombing," or any other kind of mayhem. The charges now refer to the fact that he trained and conspired with al-Qaida to harm American interests whenever and wherever he could. Whether the trial will commence as scheduled is an open question. The government has already asked that it be allowed to introduce evidence that Padilla's defense would not be permitted to examine in advance, for "national security reasons." The possibilities for delay are endless, as are the possibilities of result.

The case might end in an acquittal as some terrorism cases have; the jury might deadlock as some have; it might be thrown out by the judge as some have; it might end in a plea-bargain with the court giving Padilla credit for "time-served," Padilla relinquishing his right to appeal, and the government promising never to restore "enemy combatant" status; finally, it might end in a straightforward conviction as some have, and, if it does, it might produce an appeal as almost all have.[97] If appealed, it would normally go to the 4th

---

[96] Linda Greenhouse, "Justices let U.S. transfer Padilla," N.Y.Times, Jan. 5, 2006.
[97] In the two years from 9/11 the Department of Justice listed 6,400 terrorism-related items. The data following is drawn from DOJ figures as analyzed by the Transactional Records Access Clearinghouse (TRAC) affiliated with Syracuse University. TRAC reports that federal investigators recommended 6,400 people for terrorist-related trials to the 94 U.S. Attorneys. Of those, 1554 were not prosecuted, 2845 were being considered at the time of TRAC's report, and 879 had been convicted. Of those convicted, 373 received prison time: 263 were sentenced to "time already served pending trial," 30 received home detention, 23 were referred to drug and/or alcohol abuse programs, and 17 to mental health programs. The median prison term was 14 days, although 5 of the 373 received 20

Circuit Court of Appeal once more and, if appealed from there, to the Supreme Court once more. I would lay money on the plea-bargain, which would avoid all this. Only two things seem certain: (1) Padilla will remain in jail pending and during trial, and (2) the Bush Administration will use any and every stratagem to avoid having to defend its essentially indefensible actions in still another appearance before the Supreme Court of the United States.

What must not be lost sight of, is the fact that the Padilla Case, after four years, finally reached the normal *beginning* stage of a criminal trial. It reached this stage solely due to a process that commenced with the filing of one petition for a writ of habeas corpus by Donna R. Newman on behalf of Jose Padilla before Judge Mukasey's Federal District Court in 2002. The case has engaged the attention of the President, the Secretary of Defense, two Attorney-Generals, three Federal District Courts, two Circuit Courts of Appeal, the Supreme Court, and a host of contending attorneys. All this on the account of a man who, in the end, turns out to be a very low-level, dispensable, and incompetent recruit of an admitted enemy of the United States. In the 800-year history of habeas corpus there are few, if any, more compelling illustrations of the writ's importance in preserving an open system "with liberty and justice for all."

Looking Forward, Looking Back: As of this writing in June 2006, it seems that the courts are gradually and cautiously rejecting President Bush's "all-the-world's-a-battlefield" approach, with the American president as Commander-in-Chief. Why he is so insistent on elevating exigency and expediency to the level of constitutionality remains a mystery, but what is clear is that his reasoning on these matters eviscerates all sections of the Constitution save Article II, the Presidential article. I can think of

---

years or more. There are problems with the DOJ classifications – for example, of the 35 "terror cases" in Iowa one involved five Mexican laborers who stole baby food and sold it to a man of Arab descent for later resale. Prosecutors in Iowa and elsewhere were clearly responding to DOJ pressure to build-up the terrorism statistics. Nationwide, the cases range from silly ones like the one mentioned to the deadly serious like that of Richard Reid, the shoe bomber.

no approach more corrosive to the nation's traditional constitutional and legal order.

Supreme Court Justice Antonin Scalia took both the administration and some of his fellow-justices to task for lacking in basic honesty and failing to enforce obvious constitutional prescriptions. Dissenting in the case Hamdi v. Rumsfeld, 542 U.S. 507 (2004), he pointed out that the Constitution already provides a way of dealing with a U.S. citizen who aids an enemy – an indictment and trial for treason.[98] This would occur before the ordinary federal courts with the usual protections. Nowhere does the Constitution authorize the President to imprison citizens at his pleasure, however nasty that citizen might be. Further, he noted that if an extreme case, such as invasion, called for extreme, temporary measures, then the Congress can suspend the writ of habeas corpus. In the ultimate situation, if the President or events persuade the American people and their Congress (the first branch of government) of the dangers, then the President (the second branch of government) will be able to secure a Congressional declaration of war and a suspension of the writ of habeas corpus. Then the President can declare martial law and do all the things that are currently being done illegally, within the law and without interference from the courts (the third branch of government). The administration would have no need for end runs, double talk, and cheap litigation tricks.

Justice Scalia also scolded his fellow justices for trying to "save" President Bush's policies and tactics by using courts to "fix" illegal administrative action. In his view, if the President cannot make the political case, or if his Attorney General cannot make a specific legal case, then they, of all government officials, should abide by the existing Constitutional and legal system, one that abhors arbitrary, unchecked executive power. As matters stood in 2004 Justices Scalia and Stevens were of the uncompromising

---

[98] For unexplained reasons, the Bush Administration has been unwilling to seek treason indictments in terror cases, even when they seemed easily supportable, for example, in the case of John Walker Lindh. The government charged him in a ten count indictment that listed almost everything but treason, and that indictment served as the basis of a plea-bargain.

opinion that the government's detentions of citizens without trial should be declared unconstitutional.[99]

From 2004 to the present, it does appear that a court majority has embarked upon a less principled, less coherent, more stressful and incremental approach to reach a similar result. The stress within the Court was clearly indicated in the judgment issued on Decision Monday, April 3, 2006, rejecting Padilla's appeal from the opinion of the 4th Circuit, to the effect that President Bush could imprison him and throw away the keys. Supreme Court rules require a minimum of four justices to vote for hearing an appeal; Padilla's appeal mustered only three. Of these three only one, Justice Ginsburg explained her position, the remaining two, Justices Souter and Breyer, did not. Six justices voted against hearing the appeal. Of those, three (Kennedy, Roberts, Stevens) agreed with an explanation of their negative vote written by Justice Kennedy. The other three (Scalia, Alito, Thomas) gave no reason. Even this final decision "not to hear" took much longer than is usually the case.

Another indication of stress lay in the fact that JJ. Kennedy, Roberts, and Stevens, in explaining their vote, included a pointed reminder to the President that Padilla was entitled to all normal defendant's rights and, more importantly, that the federal courts stood ready to intervene "...were the government to seek to change the status or conditions of Padilla's custody." In many years of studying public law cases, I have never before seen a direct warning from Supreme Court justices to a sitting President predicting what the Court would do *in the future* if he continued to act as he had in the past. It is clear that the bitter complaints from J. Luttig and the 4th Circuit were heard. The Padilla Case is proving the old legal adage that "Hard cases make bad law."

From the viewpoint of the development of habeas corpus, perhaps the most interesting aspect of the Padilla Case is that the current arguments relating to executive power, judicial authority, and individual rights clearly echo those that produced the Resolution of the Judges in 1592 and Darnell's Case in 1627.[100] Even the

---

[99] Justice Antonin Scalia in dissent (joined by J. Stevens) in Hamdi v. Rumsfeld, 542 U.S. 507 (2004).

[100] See pp. 39 et seq. for the Resolution, pp.59 et seq. for Darnell's.

response of King Charles I to those who criticized his extraordinary use of the royal prerogative – "Trust Me" – has a contemporary ring. The King won his case before King's Bench, but lost the political war that the case jump-started. The loss of that war cost him his anointed head and opened a new era in English political development. It also gave birth to habeas corpus as the Writ of Liberty. It remains to be seen how President George W. Bush's restatement of the royal position will fare, or what will be it's long-term impact on the American constitution.

In his defense of the proposed federal constitution, Alexander Hamilton pointed out that it contained the essential provisions needed by citizens to protect themselves from arbitrary government, namely, the right to a jury trial and the right to petition for a writ of habeas corpus. He believed that these two provisions, by themselves, were adequate to guarantee a free citizenry – the essential underpinning of any republic.[101] Perhaps agreeing, James Madison did not include habeas corpus in his drafts of the Bill of Rights, nor did it appear, after debate, in the final twelve that were submitted to the states. As noted earlier, it never made the transition to the exalted level of a "natural right of man," but was considered essential to the protection of them.

Thomas Jefferson, in his correspondence from France, thought the omission a serious mistake, and in letters to Madison and others made suggestions like the following: "I like [the declaration of rights] as far as it goes, but I should have been for going further. For instance, the following alterations and additions would have pleased me..... Article 8. No person shall be held in confinement more than ___ days after he shall have demanded and been refused a writ of habeas corpus by the judge appointed by law, nor more than ___ days after such writ shall have been served on the person holding him in confinement, and no order [having been]

---

[101] The Federalist Papers No. 84

given on due examination for his remandment or discharge, nor more than ___ hours in any place of a greater distance than ___ miles from the usual residence of some judge authorized to issue a writ of habeas corpus; nor shall the writ be suspended for any term exceeding one year, nor in any place more than ___ miles distant from the "State or encampment of enemies or insurgents."[102]

This was not a political speech praising liberty, it was a practical, working draft embodying the experience and common sense of the 18th century. If anything like Jefferson's suggestion had been incorporated, it is unlikely that our national history would record Japanese-American concentration camps, a Guantanamo military prison, and a president ordering the imprisonment of an American citizen without charge or trial. Perhaps it is time to seriously consider Jefferson's proposals as an amendment to our Constitution.

The leaders of our Revolutionary and Constitutional periods had fought in struggles against arbitrary rulers and they understood their heritage much better and more immediately than is common today. They knew that Cicero's famous maxim "Inter arma enim silent leges" (in time of war the law falls silent) while true, could never apply fully in a republic, for a republic must always find a working balance between security and liberty. It cannot permit the law to fall silent, for as the law falls so does the republic, and the government of laws regresses to one of men.

As usual Ben Franklin said it best: "Any society that would give up a little liberty to gain a little security will deserve neither and lose both." Would that all our leaders today had that understanding and be of such calibre, but short of that, we must rely on our own "eternal vigilance...", lawyers and judges of independence and courage, as well as such time-tested tools as habeas corpus, the Writ of Liberty, to guide and guard us through a dangerous 21st century.

---

[102] Thomas Jefferson to James Madison, 1789, *The Writings of Thomas Jefferson, Memorial Edition* (Washington, D.C. 1903), vol. 7, p. 450.

INDEX

Habeas Corpus form on flyleaf:

The King to the sheriff, greetings.
We Command you to distrain "A"
of his lands and cattle in your bailiwick,
and to have his body before the court of Our justices,
on such day, to respond to "B."